D1737889

*Water Shining Beyond the Fields*

## Other Books by John Brandi

*In What Disappears*
WHITE PINE PRESS

*Reflections in the Lizard's Eye*
WESTERN EDGE PRESS

*One Cup and Another*
TANGRAM PRESS

*Stone Garland*
TOOTH OF TIME BOOKS

*A Question of Journey*
LIGHT AND DUST BOOKS

*Unmasking the Fire*
with Renée Gregorio
YOO-HOO PRESS

*No Other Business Here*
with Steve Sanfield
LA ALAMEDA PRESS

*John Brandi*

# WATER SHINING BEYOND THE FIELDS

## HAIBUN TRAVELS SOUTHEAST ASIA

TRES CHICAS BOOKS

Grateful acknowledgment to the editors of the
*Kyoto Journal*, Kyoto, Japan, and *The Global Anthology*, Glasgow, Scotland,
where sections of this book previously appeared. The journeys
presented herein were originally published in limited-edition,
hand-bound xerox editions by Tooth of Time Books, New Mexico.
Thanks to readers and libraries who supported these editions
through purchases or donations.

Thanks to Stephen Finn and Sharon Philpott
who kindly supported the production of this book.

Book Design: Renée Gregorio & JB Bryan
Cover design: JB Bryan
Cover photograph by Renée Gregorio

ISBN: 1-893003-09-4

Tres Chicas Books
P.O. Box 417
El Rito, New Mexico 87530

*Each step is an arrival. Forget about past walking,*
*don't think about future walking. One step, another step.*
*No long ago, no now, no east or west. One step equals totality.*
FAYAN WENYI
(885–958)

# CONTENTS

WHEREVER WE ARE, THIS IS OUR FUEL...

Wandering: an Act of Renunciation & of Solidarity. TRAVELING: a PRACTICE & a process, neither for escape nor entertainment, in which one seeks source & Renewal in the inevitable mysteries of place & people. Pilgrimage: symbolic hoedown. A way of life, of poetry. A conspiracy that sabotages headlines with truth.

## BY WAY OF ENTRY

Since boyhood I've been obsessed with writing down incidents of travel, the notations gathering speed in the Sixties when I lived in the Andes as a Peace Corps volunteer. In 1979 I took my first journey to India, inspired by my father's travels during the 1940s and my own need to feed from a place which represented the antithesis of the Americas. Since then the pendulum has carried me back to Asia many times, particularly Southeast Asia. The writings in this book were recorded on three separate journeys with my wife, Renée Gregorio, during the years 2001–2004.

Journaling has always played a role in my home life and especially in travels, but it was not until the late 1990s that the prose snippets in my journals began to find themselves punctuated by, or separated by, haiku. I made no conscious effort toward this form, yet found my practice of poetry, travel jottings, and haiku merging quite naturally as I strode forth in my explorations of new places, new peoples.

Matsuo Bashō (1644–94), was the great master of haiku and of the poetic pilgrimage. "Traveler is my name," he wrote, as he wandered Japan on foot, his life and poetry fed by the particulars of solitude, lack of material belongings, camaraderie with the working class, and intimacy with the natural world. Taking to the road after re-energizing the haiku form, he wrote several travel journals and an extended diary in the haibun style of linked poetry and prose (vivid, descriptive, imagistic prose punctuated by haiku). His most famous work, written at the very end of his life, and the crowning masterpiece of the haibun form, was *Oku no hosomichi* (*Narrow Road to the Interior*).

Kobayashi Issa (1762-1826) also wrote haibun, his most famous being his autobiography: *Ora ga haru* (*Spring of my Life*). In North America, Jack Kerouac explored the form. Section 28, in *Desolation Angels* (1965), a personal favorite, is a quick prose snippet describing a lightning storm in the northern Cascades from Kerouac's fire lookout. In it, he makes an amazing leap from universal to personal—the hiss, tick, and booming flash of the storm to maternal affection. His energetic prose description of the storm ends with:

> Thunder in the mountains—
> the iron
> Of my mother's love.

As haiku and haibun reached other continents, their Japanese forms mutated into new variations with each geographic and linguistic encounter. Haibun might traditionally be regarded as a series of in situ prose descriptions (sans metaphor, abstraction, generalization), each of them concluded by a haiku. I have often thought that a function of the haiku might be to punctuate the prose, i.e., revealing an unexpected flash, core, essence, of what the prose didn't quite capture or describe. The haiku thus becomes a kind of imagistic, miniature, sixth-sense portrait of something not described in the prose; something unexpectedly essential that eye-ear-nose-taste-touch did not reveal. But I didn't set out to follow any rules, my own or Bashō's; I set out to set out. In re-reading the text I find that sometimes the final line of the prose didn't want to stay put; it jumped into three short lines instead.

These journeys were recorded as they unrolled, details usually scribbled in spiral pocketbooks on a bus, in a temple corner, cliff hopping, riding a bike, rambling markets, or ducking under a veranda in the rain. Late evening or next morning, crosslegged on the floor, in a cafe, or on a rare chair before a desk, the scribbled prose blocks, with occasional haiku in between, would be transferred to a larger notebook. At home, after travels, I took to transcribing the journals. Donkey work at times, but mostly a pleasurable chance to relive the journey and discover where, exactly, I had been—from a comfortable distance. The biggest effort was to remain true to the notebooks, the immediacy of the firsthand "takes"—no alterations to remake the travels into something they weren't.

I would like to thank Stephen Finn and Sharon Philpott for their continuing support of my work, and Renée Gregorio for her hard work and valuable insight in helping me shape this book.

**john brandi**
*el rito, nm: 4.vii.05*

TA SOM: CAMBODIA
a stately ficus
bends skyward
in
dramatic
surge.
The sun
is vitreous,
the odor
sweet,
exotic,
Ambrosial.

Thick
naga roots
slither along
galleries, through
cracks, over stone
roofs, everything
solid now un-
dulating:
a slow motion
earthquake,
everything
stooped &
heaving in
filtered light.
Green light.

Paths buckle, stone walls
collapse, a goddess
blinks as lichened fish
nibble her toes.

# CAMBODIA
## ANGKOR WAT & PHNOM PENH

*Months and days are eternal travelers,*
*the passing years are travelers too*
BASHŌ
(1689)

Turbo prop out of Bangkok into pale green cloud scud to Cambodia. Short flight. Nevertheless, we're served guava juice, sandwich, dessert with spring water, and a potent hit of coffee. "My mom flew all the way across America and all she got was peanuts," Renée laughs. "And I bet she didn't get these kind of smiles," I add. Half hour later, the land unrolls into steeply wooded hills, then drops into the emerald Cambodian plain broken only by scattered phnoms—abrupt mounds thick with vegetation. Most likely these were temples in their own right, sacred to animist cultures long before Hindus arrived in the first century and placed their gods on them. Not much human activity below, until we lower into Siem Reap where palms and wood-stilt houses line dusty roads that trail into the murky Tonle Sap, at its highest this month. A poignancy fills my psyche as we lower through broken mists—same feeling I had as we landed in Vietnam a few years ago. To be driven here by the desire to visit Angkor is to confront the presence of ghosts, recent horrors of civil war, aftermath of genocide, the two million missing who died under the Khmer Rouge—all inseparable from the quest.

The little airport is quiet, the officials polite. With ease we obtain a 30-day visa. Siem Reap, a town once sacked and destroyed by the Khmer Rouge, is now experiencing a hammering tourist boom. There's relative political stability; most of the land mines have been cleared (even one stray is too many); roads are opening up; hotels, restaurants, tour agencies are mushrooming. After Cambodia's civil war and the death of Pol Pot in '97, anyone who's ever dreamed of Angkor Wat is headed here. It's an old dream for me. It began with Allen Ginsberg's poem "in a stone nook in the rain/Avalokitesvara faces everywhere" (1963), and quickly escalated after visiting Palenque; then, through the decades: Varanasi's river shrines, Borobudur in Java, Pagan on the Irrawaddy, Bodhnath in Nepal. Now, for my 60th birthday, it's time for Angkor Wat. Ironic, choosing Cambodia as a place to mark this passage, but I've had enough of the paranoid Bush regime at home, moving into totalitarianism at breakneck speed, suspecting anyone who has the capacity to think or act outside the corporate box as a "terrorist threat." I'll blow out my candles elsewhere, thank you.

Off Wat Bo Street—a neighborhood of leafy trees, potholed lanes, stilt houses, hairdressers, fruit stands, guest houses, shop-house variety stores, and an impeccably arranged auto-parts shop—we settle into the Khmer-owned "Home Sweet Home." $15 a night with a/c, hot water, wood floors, writing desk. Easy walk to Psar Chas (central market) and to several excellent Khmer restaurants. Only six kilometers to the ruins, so we'll be able to rise early, explore until it gets hot, return for lunch and nap, resume our exploration in the afternoon. Out front, a cyclo driver sleeps in his plastic-fringed trishaw painted with two pink doves above silver script:

EVERY TIME IS HAPPY

We meet Ponheary Ly, our guide to Angkor for the next two days, an energetic 41-year-old Khmer woman, unmarried, free spirited, a sharp thinker who speaks English, French, and Russian. We pass the afternoon in soft, animated conversation. Little by little, we learn of her suffering during the Khmer Rouge: how she and her family were forced from their village into a wat (temple compound) converted into a labor camp; how her father, a teacher, was killed with dozens of other teachers; how she survived on food hidden in trees by sympathetic villagers; how she was caught "stealing" food, asked to dig her own grave, clubbed and left for dead, before finally escaping.

After Ponheary leaves, we head to the entrance of Angkor for our $60 one-week pass. We have our photos taken, wait, then receive them laminated on the official entrance ticket: stamped, numbered, dated. That done, we hop on waiting motorbikes and are driven to Phnom Bakheng for sunset, a ninth-century Shiva temple on a 70-meter hill a bit northwest of the famous Angkor Wat. Immediately it hits us how vast and densely forested the place is, even without the many stately trees that have been logged. Angkor Wat is only one of dozens of stone monuments here, but its name often refers to the entire 77 square miles of archeology in the Unesco world heritage site.

Beyond the entrance gate, we aren't alone. Hoards of people are streaming in. Travelers from the world's 26,000 corners; Siem Reap locals; Cambodians from distant provinces, dressed in white, quite striking against the backdrop of ivy-green. Under spreading canopies of leaves, people arrive on bikes, motos, cyclos, buses, cars, or by foot, slapping along on flip-flops. Entire extended families unwrap picnic baskets, rice wine, skewers of meat, and sweets. Between the trees, they spread out on mats around braziers, glasses, banana-leaf plates, Chinese thermoses. It's Sunday, the mood festive. I want to mind the people but don't. It's suddenly like India, a living temple, not some remnant of the bygone. Construction workers, too, pedal along, shortcutting through the ruins to their villages—families who crush rock and haul cement at $1.50 a day, faces wrapped with kramas, the red and white checkered scarves the Khmer Rouge adopted as part of their look.

Most visitors are here to climb Phnom Bakheng, which is exactly what we're doing. Stretching legs up huge steps smoothed by centuries of feet, sweep of monsoons, idle free fall of tropical leaves, and the nightly passing of spirits. Up, up. It's one collective human effort, an ant parade of travelers groping through thick lavender heat: the puppet of pleasure in her red windbreaker, a historian with tripod stool, a Bombay grandma in neon-blue, a juggler from Liverpool, an Australian with orange mustache and film-weighted vest, the doll-like Chinese who smell of willow wood, a falling-behind trio of Kuala Lumpur men in silk dinner jackets, a wonder-eyed French boy whose tap-dance heels leave flames. All amid a trail of pungency: someone's humid underarms, a bit of Opium, Essence of Jaipur, even a hint of hash smoke. I step around a Japanese girl who insists on an umbrella, even though there's no rain and it's almost dark. A Khmer couple prattles and cuddles. A monk effortlessly levitates past them. There he goes, up the old Hindu hill: young and dapper, shaved head, cinnamon skin, flowing saffron robe accentuated with bright purple towel wrapped around his neck.

Finally, the summit, where I turn not toward the ruins or sunset, but to the circus-like faces dreamily staring at the spongy horizon of temple tops silhouetted against a fat crimson sun. Gong-like, it disappears into the raised arms of a lone tree jutting from the forest. A few water vendors are hanging out, children mostly; and a woman hawking pirated guides to the ruins. Even at this hour the heat is high, the humidity strong:

> the postcard seller
> folds out all ten views
> and fans herself.

Back down in semi-darkness, we step level to level, passing stone towers on each of five tiers cut from the hill. Joss sticks burn in firefly clusters. Two musicians, barely visible in the gnarled woods, play upright fiddles. Another patters a twin-headed drum. A fuzzy silhouette comes into focus, puts a leaf to lips, joins in with a reed man on shenai-like clarinet. High-pitched singing, clang of finger cymbals. All of it—the hazy air, moist warmth, our own exhaustion—puts us in an intoxicated state. In the parking lot, where taxis and cyclos wait, is another group of musicians. In front of their strumming, a boy rattles a plastic alms cup:

> night deepens
> after I discover
> the singer's blind eyes.

Siem Reap. We eat dinner at the Bayon Restaurant, a short walk from our inn. Ice-cold Angkor beer, amok (Tonle Sap fish bathed in curry served in coconut shell), steamed rice, lemongrass soup, and longan for dessert—brown-skinned tropical grapes with pearly-sweet flesh. A shadow-puppet performance follows. By comparison, those in Bali are more professional. Here, puppeteers and chorus are young teenage boys and girls, accompanied by a much older maestra who provides part of the dialogue. Perhaps before the Khmer Rouge killed so many of the country's performers, the role of the teenagers had been that of adults. The musicians are especially good, backing the troupe on gong chimes, xylophone, hourglass drum, upright drum, metal clappers, and two very primitive oboe/clarinet-like instruments.

## 27 OCTOBER: SIEM REAP

7 A.M. sharp. Ponheary fetches us. We're off to Angkor Wat, entering from the east, not the usual tourist route, west. It's quiet, nobody around. For three hours we meander the immense, ancient complex hidden behind walls approached by a long stone causeway bordered with serpent balustrades. The bridge to the main entrance—which we tour later at sunset and sunrise—spans an 800-foot-wide moat that wraps the entire temple (about 3.5 miles). Inside the walls is a labyrinth of covered galleries, chambers, towers, ceremonial platforms, and courtyards—all on different levels, unbelievably ornamented. If viewed from the air it would be easy to discern a mandala-like plan, but from the ground, it's difficult. Angkor Wat is a cosmogram whose central towers represent the peaks of Mt. Meru, axis of the Hindu universe, home of the gods. Around them are arranged the continents, represented by the vaulted galleries containing the famous bas reliefs. Then come the outer walls, symbolic of the mountain ranges at the world's edge—and of the successive stages of knowledge. Finally, there is the moat, the cosmic ocean. When you cross it, you leave behind the world of the profane and step into the esoteric stages of the arcane.

Narratives depicting Hindu myths adorn the inner galleries: architecture as storybook, the "pages" exquisitely carved on two meter-high walls, the detail minute. Picture stones, to be read horizontally—clockwise. "The Churning of the Milk Ocean" is our favorite. I've read translations of this story, seen episodes in New Delhi street plays, found bits and pieces of its sculptured heroes in world museums. Now the story leaps off the wall in front of us: gods and demons oppose each other, pulling on a great rope (the cosmic serpent) to churn amrita, the elixir of immortality, into the world. Not only do they succeed, they froth into existence Laxmi, wife of Vishnu; along with the moon god; a celestial conch; and dozens of erotic apsaras, heavenly dancers whose fingers flutter with secret mudras.

The apsaras float across the wall in dreamy trance, with sumptuous breasts and diaphanous outfits, heads adorned with flame-like tiaras. Their rapturous eyes and smiles evoke a state of communing with the Other, a hearing of a voice, a music, rarely permitted into the human ear. Some of the smiles indicate blissful satisfaction, as if the dancers had just completed a successful telling of their stories with feet, hips, and hands (I think of the lingering afterglow that an actor, poet, or composer feels after a climactic storm of creation). Finally, there are half-parted lips that convey transience, a whisper emerging from a celestial realm. These are the apsaras who look you in the eye from earth-warmed stone and say: stop, tremble awe,

> there's a world
> behind this world we rake
> with plows.

After the galleries of bas reliefs, we ascend the heart of Angkor: Mt. Meru. Up steep stone stairs into dark galleries, each with Buddha, attendant, coin box, incense urn. With a view over the entire magic mountain, we end our morning pleasantly exhausted, a bow and a prayer for loved ones. As we leave for lunch, Ponheary stands before a bas relief of a king humbling a woman on a bed of arrows. "The story is that he did that to demonstrate his power, to show his strength. But he should have sacrificed his power to show his strength, not the woman. That would have made the world better." We talk about world leaders, their inability to dissolve their egos, conquer their own greed. Ponheary punctuates the discussion with her thought about war:

> "even if you win
> you have the word
> 'lost' inside."

At 3 P.M. we return to the ruins. This time to Angkor Thom, the expansive temple-city beyond Angkor Wat, approached by a stone causeway that leads through a much-photographed gopura (gate) in the wall, topped by giant Bodhisattva faces smiling into the four directions. These tall, narrow entranceways are truly majestic. Their corbeled arches are crowned with symbols, their sculpted thresholds rising nearly 70 feet. The centuries have embellished the stone with tropical growth, enhancing its already exotic presence. We linger, examining the twin serpent (naga) rails bordering the causeway. Each of the snakes curves into nine raised heads, while on their bodies ride 54 gods (left) and 54 demons (right), totaling 108, the number of prayer beads you'd find on a Buddhist rosary. The gods and demons are actually the main characters from the "The Churning of the Milk Ocean." On the other side of the gopura, the causeway becomes a road leading straight through a jungle once filled with wooden houses for royal families, priests, and military officials—all eaten away by time.

At the center of Angkor Thom is Bayon, a rambling, wildly baroque 12th-century temple crowned with huge, smiling Avalokitesvara faces said to resemble the king who commissioned them. Bayon is an auspicious place, the exact geographical center of Angkor Thom, a stone heart still beating. Silvery, almost metallic in the fuzzy afternoon light, the whole place vibrates with auras, shadow images, a timbre of its own. We don't enter right away, but hold back to ponder the reflections in a tree-draped moat. A quiet, timeless moment. Monks chanting in a wat half hidden in the trees; a cowherd driving her buffaloes into a grassy marsh, where they sink and raise their shiny noses from a maze of floating lilies.

Inside the walls, the enigmatic heads—more than 200 of them—stare into space from their stone towers. Under them, we examine bas reliefs, not as intricate as those of Angkor Wat, but more deeply carved so the pictures are easier to see. The artists obviously enjoyed rendering these explicit scenes from everyday life: market goers bargaining, fishermen lowering nets, wrestlers flexing, acrobats juggling, a princess surrounded by suitors, a woman giving birth, a meditating sadhu treed by tigers. There are also the inevitable military battles. "It's all about war," a friend who had visited Angkor told us: "battles from Hindu myths, battles fought by ancient kings, battles with the Khmer Rouge that left thousands maimed, many whom you will see begging in the ruins."

By evening, we're ready to collapse. The heat, Renée's period coming on, lingering jet lag, the walking, climbing, and sensory input. En route to dinner, we stop at the corner of Wat Bo and Avenue 6 to watch passing tire whiz of rickshaws, motos, and bikes transporting pigs in bamboo cages; spirit houses; bald red-robed monks; bald white-robed nuns; families packed six to a scooter, hens on handlebars, coconuts in saddlebags, crutches, bananas, roof thatch tied to crossframes; smiling apsara schoolgirls; framed portraits of the king; a toilet; a bundle of sugar cane; a sick man on a motorbike, i.v. being fed into his arm by a nurse holding onto him from behind while holding the serum bottle above.

We retire at 8 P.M. after a $6.50-for-two dinner at Arun Guest House. Crab soup, shrimp spring rolls, rice, and papaya dessert. A family-run place whose members stood near us like buddhas during the entire meal—an old world attention and courtesy that brought tears to our eyes; it's so missing in today's world. A note attached to the menu made us laugh:

"also have
fresh
crap salad."

## 28 OCTOBER: SIEM REAP

We review our morning at Angkor over beer and lunch in the cool courtyard of Sawasdee restaurant, Thai food served by a courteous staff of young girls wrapped in shimmering blue. Ponheary took us first to Prasat Kravan, the Cardamom Sanctuary, a small ruin with Vishnu and Laxmi sculpted from darkened brick interiors. Intimate place, easy to like, sweet waft of joss sticks from smoking urn above yoni pedestal. Green foliage behind, cresting into blue, post-monsoon sky. I wasn't totally in tune with the red brick, though; still filled with yesterday's bas reliefs on golden stone: sculpted fish swimming from finely carved nets enhanced by centuries of spreading moss, red mineral stains, the oily fingers of passing worshipers—farmers, innocent school kids, and not-so-innocent tourists. My notes read:

"Third-eye full, yet thirsty for more. Knapsack sweaty against spine, diary fat with scribbles and sidetracks. The inherent urge: assemble these mind ramblings, building blocks, deep-down sidetracks, eyeball reality rotations; carve them into pictures; find the narrative. Wonder if that's not me that the crocodile's ready to swallow on the bas reliefs? The scruffy, tangled-in-thought ascetic floating on lotus leaf."

Srah Srang was our next stop, a 12th-century ceremonial bathing lake. A quiet, meditative place. Men and women clearing the water of weeds, up to their knees in reflections, circled by dragonflies. Hard, stifling work—despite the beauty—in such heat and muck. "Too poor in education for other work," Ponheary said. "Still, at about $1.50 a day, they can get by." Her eyes were glassy as she pondered the curved, sweating backs. Silence followed, until I spoke, uncomfortably. "You're lucky to have this job as guide." "Yes, but I've suffered, we've all suffered. I did that kind of labor before being lucky." Our talk turns to the

Khmer Rouge. About hungry people fleeing endless American bombs. About these same hungry peasants, battered and given up, being swayed toward hate and ruthlessness as a sense of empowerment. But even this is too simplistic.

"Everybody wants to know how it could happen," Ponheary says. "Don't ask me how it happened, I have no answer. All I can tell you is the history, the rest I can't explain." She tells a story about how her aunt was killed by the Khmer Rouge. "She was rounded up with all those thought to be 'suspicious' and taken to a labor camp, and then separated from her lover" (the KR's policy was to break up pairs, to destroy family units, to send mothers, fathers, children, grandparents to separate camps). "In her new camp, she was lined up with other women next to men who had suffered a similar fate. The KR pulled people out of the lines at random and 'married' them. My aunt and her new partner pretended to be married during the day, but at night they secretly went off to their real partners. They did this until a spy reported their 'treachery' to the KR, who stood them in front of others as an example of disobedience. 'We're going to marry you again—for life,' the KR said. 'But only after you're dead.' They were executed on the spot."

Banteay Kdei. Our favorite temple, after Bayon. A bit fallen in, but beautiful as such. A monastic complex with learning sanctuary, libraries, and "Hall of Dancing Girls"—named by archeologists because of a frieze of dancers overlooking the terrace. When the guards disappear (they're usually sleeping), I privately kiss a sun-warmed apsara before rejoining Renée and Ponheary in the next gallery. Once, the forest would not let these temples escape; now the woods are trimmed daily. Still, moss ascends a staircase, red-lichened fish nibble the toes of a tumbled angel, roots groan as they split ancient walls carved with Sanskrit into piecemeal script. Moist temples that nursed huge banyans skyward, and held them there, are now held in place by those same giant banyans who wrap their tendons around them. Buddhist monks studied here. Later, new generations of Hindu kings hacked out Buddha's eyes. Wild deer browsed the overgrown learning halls. Then came the archeologists, then the Khmer Rouge:

> in the heat
> a hawk dropping
> where dragonflies play.

Nearby is Ta Prohm, another Buddhist monastery, the monument that most evokes the mystery of Angkor. French archaeologists left this one pretty much as found: overgrown, surreal like an Ernst or Dali painting. Giant ficus and kapok trees rise into the sky from the stone. Parrots squawk in leafy canopies. Tourists squawk, too. Japanese and Chinese, mainly, in quick-moving groups. Between their boisterous visits, though, pleasantly long periods go by without a soul:

> the silence—
> dry leaves falling
> into blooming grasses.

Instead of the usual carved-serpent balustrades, here we find living trees forming the balustrades. Thick naga roots slither along galleries, through cracks, into dank chambers, over stone roofs—dislodging lintels and toppling columns. Broken apart this way, the former grace and order of the architecture has slipped into chaos. What was once solid and evenly laid out now undulates as if in a slow-motion earthquake. Stooped and heaving in filtered green light, the moats and courtyards designed to represent space and time are distorted into compositions of contradiction and conflict. There are partial views, blocked doorways, tumbled-in gardens, haunted dead ends, fragmented glimpses that the builders never intended. Terraces ideal for fixed meditation now writhe with the movement of the universe. Paths buckle as sinewy fingers of chlorophyll crawl beneath them. Wait a few centuries, and one unexpected day there's a shift, a tumble. Rain, seeping moisture, the pull of gravity do their work:

> stone vaults collapse
> roof becomes sky, stars shine
> from rain pools.

## 28 OCTOBER: SIEM REAP

Dinner near the old market, a place called Taj Mahal. Malai kofta, garlic nan, masala dosa, mango lassi, assorted chutneys, syrup-smothered sweet-milk pastries washed down with cardamom tea. On the way here we stopped at the Red Piano for cold beer, served by a Khmer waitress whose mudra eyes drugged our own and soothed the psyche with a little amrita against further news of war: the U.S. cowardly putting its claws around its chosen foe, a defenseless one, at that. Camus once wrote: "The most incorrigible vice is that of an ignorance which fancies it knows everything and therefore claims for itself the right to kill."

I take refuge in the smile of my beloved and drink to peace among Khmer voices, the horsy gargle of two Germans, a fast, high-pitch run of Japanese from three women looking very tiny in the Red Piano's huge stuffed chairs. "What do you remember?" I ask Renée. "Windows looking into windows. Niches emptied of Buddhas. Apsaras, each with a singular personality. A lizard looking out of a hairpiece. Vishnu napping on a wailing dragon. Butterfly fluttering from Laxmi's shoulder. Musician keeping time on a missing leg. Missing eyes raised in song. Leaf between a man's lips, his teeth gone. A collapsed stupa pink with periwinkles. Children on broken towers at sunset. A boy under a three-headed elephant clapping mosquitoes,

> a girl with a twig
> giving Buddha
> a pedicure."

A TV monitor in the corner is on, but there is no sound, just moving mouths, indications of tension, diplomacy, scourge, demand, more talk, retaliation. It's all old news, the wheel come round again. The men in uniforms and pressed suits (there are no women) look deflated. Their war on civil liberties, ignorance of cultures, disdain for history, and pithy eagerness to undo the laws that protect our air, water, and food—it's all predatory, disdainful slop in the world's bucket. We order more tea, look over our notes from this afternoon.

31

Ta Som: quiet, unrestored place. Tangled sun-drenched lianas, fallen stone. Ponheary leaves us mostly on our own to imagine, to wander, to awe. A stately ficus bends a massive trunk skyward, no branches to interrupt its dramatic surge. Otherworldly, it seems balanced on, but not attached to, the stone roof that nurtures it. The sun doesn't completely burn through the moist shade here. Growth is turbulent, the odor herbal. A sweet, exotic rot. Locusts whine among broken eaves and fallen porticoes:

> not the gods
> but the banyans
> preside.

Preah Khan. A monastery deep in the trees. Wild feeling, jungle untamed. A thousand monks once studied here. Now silent sanctuaries struggle under swelling trunks. Dancing Shiva has been brought to his knees by muscles of bark and water. The doe-eyed princess in deep relief is choked with sinuous roots. Tathagata images have been pulverized, not by the elements, but by Hindu kings. In one niche, Buddha is gone but his followers remain kneeling. Ponheary herself, though, is the real treat. She's come alive in this place. Elegant, in sunglasses, wearing her official khaki guide shirt wrapped in checkered scarf, she sits on footworn stone steps in the Compound of Learning. She muses, talks girl things with Renée (when I'm not around), discusses politics, the absence of wisdom of world leaders, lack of trust by Cambodians in their prime minister—a defector from the Khmer Rouge who bribed his way into the new government. "War cannot finish war. Give the people peace. Violence as retribution does not end terrorism."

She speaks of how Western views—where religion drives politics—obsess over sin, guilt, trial, punishment. "Cambodians are Buddhist, they don't see things black and white, or in terms of crime and punishment. Many Khmer Rouge were children made into soldiers by leaders. Why punish them? They should be forgiven, they should receive understanding. Our government has said to them, turn in your arms and we will pay you for them. Take the money, go back home, help your village."

This view at first surprises us, especially given Ponheary's own loss and suffering under Pol Pot (who was schooled in Paris and eventually backed by the U.S.). Most Cambodians are revulsed at the thought of resuming village life, facing neighbors at the well who executed their kin. But Renée had an insight into Ponheary's idea of repatriation without discrimination: "It embraces the fact that people can behave differently if you treat them differently." Such thinking is totally absent from the present U.S. regime, who acts with violence to shove its way into lands it wants to dominate then uses tricks to convince the people it's come to help them. Abroad, it's all guns, no talk. At home, it's lies, threats, manufactured fear, racist statements to fuel the masses. And the demand that the rest of the world "line up," become reasonable, while we ourselves become evermore unreasonable.

In Buddhism all things, whether animate or inanimate, have Buddha nature. Nobody is separate from the wasp, the raindrop, the baby on her mother's back, the weed in the ravine, the named enemy. "This is the true democratic path," our friend Nanao once spoke (he, the Japanese poet who witnessed the bombing of Nagasaki). To give equal value to all beings, even the most trivial object, even to those deemed "enemy" is to practice a democracy quite contrary to that embraced by the Christian West, which carries on with: "Are you not of greater value than many sparrows?"

"War against terrorism, why not peace against terrorism?" says Ponheary as we pass a wall with more of those missing statues:

> in the empty niche
> where Buddha sat
> bees at work.

## 29 OCTOBER: SIEM REAP

The barber pounds my back with cupped-hand massage after a $2 haircut. Classic mirrors, stamped tin ceiling, big rotating fans, gold spirit house above green swivel barber chairs on white porcelain pedestals with leather seats. A cheerful, thorough barber who seemed to know all I needed was a basic trim for the Angkor sun. He threw blue silk over me, pumped up the chair, went to work. Thankfully, he didn't give me an uneven cut like the one I got in Cuba (the barber and I had been drinking rum) or the one before, in Chichicastenango (where my gringo hair was swept neatly into a separate pile). I came away pleased, bowing profusely.

Oh, yes, and Poly, one of the girls hanging about. A pretty 20-year-old who spoke no English, but wanted Renée and I to linger, have tea, "be dad and mother" (this happened more than once in Cambodia), and peruse her photo album: friends smiling, embracing, fashioning. Pretending, we thought, to be people with brighter futures, happier pasts. We sipped tea, took photos, exchanged addresses, hugged each other, and for a moment—just a tiny fraction of a day in a life—we were "dad and mother" for her. Maybe she thought we would eventually help her obtain documents for a future not in Cambodia but in a new country, without poverty or corrupt, unpredictable leaders. How could I tell her ours wasn't the one? Maybe she should be dreaming of Canada or France or Brazil, I thought, as we meandered the dust and heat back to our hotel.

Today we relax, write, follow the river to the lively Psar Chas, check out silks, kramas, teapots, spice, and betel containers. Tomorrow we return to Angkor with Ponheary's driver, who'll take us to more remote sites. Meanwhile, I find an article in the *Bangkok Post* about Pagan, the ancient Burmese site filled with thousands of Buddhist pagodas, a place that may soon be spoiled by the Burmese government's proposal to build a 16-story "viewing tower" in the middle of it. There's hope that Unesco's refusal to fund Pagan as Burma's first world heritage site, if the plan becomes a reality, will stop this misadventure.

## 30 OCTOBER: SIEM REAP

Out through sun-slanted Khmer villages, rice fields vitreous green. Women combing their hair at wells, ox carts parked under shade trees, firewood stacked in roadside bundles. Deceptive beauty, of course. People barely get by here. There's definitely no tourist business. Everyone passes by, including us. A few youngsters sell trinkets in the ruins, but it's slim existence. There's a new school built by the Japanese. There's the ghost of the Khmer Rouge (where are the elders, artists, priests?). And there's the ghost of the Americans (they tore this country to shreds, dropping six million tons of bombs in 12 years—a war in that killed more than two million Vietnamese, Laotians, and Cambodians).

We continue 40 kilometers to Banteay Srei, a miniature 10th-century Hindu compound whose rose-sienna sandstone temples radiate a morning glow from the greenery. An intimate place, very feminine. Narrow doorways guarded by mythical figures; walls profuse with deep, floral scenes from the Ramayana; exquisite geometric scrollwork; floral fantasies. They remind me of the old wooden temple screens in Kathmandu—much of Angkor's stone doors, windows, columns, and beams replicate their lathe-turned woodwork.

Banteay Srei is on everyone's itinerary, so we don't exactly have it to ourselves. But there are periods of quiet, opportunities to photograph the architecture without people. Over one doorway is a loving portrait carved in pale sienna rock: Shiva and Parvati, the divine lovers. They are enshrined inside the hump of Shiva's sacred bull, Nandi, who stands among blooming lotuses. As I sketch it, a lilting song floats over the sanctuary wall. We listen, then follow the singing of a woman to a swept-dirt area beneath a shade tree. There are two crude wooden benches set up, but no audience. We take a seat. Six musicians—men dressed in thin pants and shirts stained with toil—sit crosslegged on a reed mat with the singer. They play zither, horizontal drum, upright fiddles, finger cymbals. One musician blows a leaf in perfect time with another on bamboo flute, his plastic leg unstrapped at his side. Mine victims, all of them, raising money for the disabled.

I'd like to know the stories of these people—where they're from, how they made it through, what it is they're playing, how they managed to carry on their musical traditions through war, persecution, trauma of hiding and fleeing. Supposedly in Phnom Penh there are performers who managed to survive, whose music goes back to the Angkorian time. There are troubadours, too, who improvise satirical lyrics about daily life or current events. Certainly they would have been the first to go under villains like the Khmer Rouge (I think of Lorca's fate under Franco; Victor Jara under Pinochet). White clouds gather on distant hills. The air is suddenly hot, the sky a guttering lamp of cerulean. Behind the reed player:

> fields shimmer
> beyond a gate
> made of reeds.

About a half-hour beyond Banteay Srei is the site of Kbal Spean. I watch the hills come closer, feel the heat thicken, and think about Angkor's temples, how they were designed to lift the emperor above the people in a kind of transcendence. He could ascend a tower (sacred mountain), stand in its crown, put his arms into the sky, become a conduit between heaven and earth, gods and humans, the arcane and mundane. Positioned as such, he was at the world's center—represented by the square platform upon which rose the tower, synonymous with Mt. Meru. Around him rotated the celestial worlds in tiers. These tiers, ascending into the heavens can also be realized the other way around: they are tiers descending from the heavens, steps upon which the tutelary gods came to earth. The Himalayas can be seen that way, too: ascending into clouds, descending from them in snowy tiers upon which the gods stepped down to awaken our spiritual search.

The mountain-rising-from-platform design also embodies the idea of genesis. Mountain as lingam, the primordial male force that penetrates the primordial female darkness to begin creation. In Hindu architecture the lingam (peak) stands erect on the square plane of the yoni (earth). In India there are yoni-lingam sculptures at sacred river confluences, in temples, under banyan trees. Always there is ritual going on about them: priests, young brides, sadhus, itinerant worshipers washing the stone phallus with oil, ghee, milk, or water, sanctified as it drips down its column. A jasmine flower may then be placed on the tip of the phallus, or a garland of marigolds draped around its base.

The stones for Angkor's temples were quarried from the hills we are about to enter. Torn from hidden energy streams in the earth, they were hauled out, carved, and assembled into the creation myths. Even before the chisel struck, the rocks would have embodied the inherent breath force, the spirit of the place from which they were taken. This area, sparse of human population, has its own sense of time. Outside the tinted window, wings of stone jut, cliffs scramble, trees shudder with insect drone. A cooling breeze; we get quieter. I imagine living long ago, then realize long ago is right now. I feel strangely in place, yet quickly remind myself of the irony: this is a place where everyone else has been severely displaced.

Our driver parks under a ramada lined with souvenir stands at the entrance to Kbal Spean, "Head of the River." From here we hike through wooded hills which eventually reveal the 11th-century Hindu site. Carved into the Siem Reap riverbed are countless lingams. They were auspiciously designed to sanctify the waters flowing from the hills to Angkor Wat, and to the rice fields. Rushing over the stone phalluses, the water receives its primordial blessing—no priests necessary. There's a presence strongly female in this shadowed ravine. The phalluses set within the river's cleft reveal an ancient reverence for the Mother. The water crowns from the mountain, gives a cry, then gathers momentum as it sings its song of worship, drawing the heart into retreat. The human world seems suddenly foreign, far off in its ruinous circumstance. I recall a line from Kenneth Patchen: "Will the lives of men turn clean?" Below, a wild rose swirls in the ebbing foam:

> whitewater—
> the swiftness of life
> banked with sorrow.

Walking the riverside, we eventually discover the light-colored gouge where looters hacked the carved images of Vishnu and Laxmi from the stone bank. Ponheary warned us of this. She was one of the last to see Vishnu and Laxmi "alive," March 2003, the day before the theft took place. During the time of the Khmer Rouge, Angkor was relatively safe from looters. The KR didn't vandalize the stone, but did far worse: they captured, tortured, and killed the "educated" who protected the stone. Now that peace has arrived, looters return to chisel away and haul out thousands of relics, many of them ending up on the foreign market, or in Bangkok art galleries with certificates to guarantee their authenticity.

## 31 OCTOBER: SIEM REAP

Sitting in one of the ruins yesterday—Bantaey Samre—I felt the full tranquillity of stone, silence, and cloud that Angkor Wat is capable of delivering. Silver grasses rustled with light under a perfect electric-blue sky. A few dragonflies rode the heat waves, and from over a stone wall, a breeze carried the laughter of village girls jumping rope. Out of the corner of my eye, a lone frangipani tree seemed to bend, drink from a pool, then lift again into the air to enjoy its solitude. Peering from my own solitude, I discovered a carved chariot wheel, the Dharma, turning in a maze of ornate designs above a temple doorway. Moments later, a blossom twirled to the pavement from that same doorway, rolled up to me, and gave a soft nod:

> old self, new
> self, still
> self.

Our journey is at an end. We revisit Bayon, then Angkor Thom's west gate. Rutted road, red dust in my ears, white sideburns, white tassels on waving weeds. I stuff scribbled notes under cap, notice Renée's sweat has turned the nape of her neck dark. At the crumbled gopura, nobody around save for a guard sleepily talking to a farmer leaning on his bike under a big banyan. Butterflies float above a trail through deep woods skirting the old city wall. We want to follow, but the place has a spooky feel. Land mines? Instead, we stroll across the crumbling causeway. The serpent balustrades have long fallen in on themselves, but there's an appeal to seeing them this way. The imperfection lends itself to the imagination. We just fill in the blanks, line the balustrades with our own mythical creatures, and between them, cross the moat on the crumbling causeway into the old, walled city—the Eden of renewed consciousness.

## 3 NOVEMBER: SIEM REAP

Bags packed, mind in the abstract beehive of what's up, where been. Tomorrow we head for Phnom Penh. Brilliant stars fill the night, children shout in the street. A bottle rocket goes bang, a little dog whines into ragtag imperfection of hanging trees, crooked balconies, the secrets we keep, the thoughts that race. My hair's up straight, my sarong wet after a cold shower. A squeaking ox cart slips from the darkness; old monk wrings his robe. Ex-pat, face like a river bottom, sits at a cyber-keyboard asking for beer refill. In the lobby, a young traveler endlessly rearranges her pack, baring a Japanese monkey that disappears into her panty line— a blue tattoo. I flare nostrils, smell guava blossoms, roof tar, wood fires, patchouli oil. The night is filled with thin dreams, cornered questions, the potent possibilities of Cambodia:

> neon signs
> over bones in the garden
> where children play.

All said and done (strange concept), it seems to me that Angkor Wat is a conduit, a lightning rod between heaven and earth, a cosmic ship mast between the moon-misted world of smiling apsaras and the mundane world of money-making in techno rat-race. Stone cities rose and fell, and continue to do so inside the psyche. The low-hung moon is red with slaughter; the golden age is dream-mulched into its own collapsible beginning. Who can be sure of anything? Reality's an ongoing slide-show of appearances and disappearances, a flimsy hello inside an eternal farewell. Thirteen centuries ago, Wang Wei asked, "Isn't it that we all live out our lives in the maze of a dream?" And Emerson, not so far back, jumped up from his gray-haired chair and exclaimed: "The sky is the daily bread of the eyes!"

So? Long live imagination! It's our raft within the chopped-up sea of typhoon and undertow, the blasphemous dictators, the stink of war that negates the sanctity of life. The rigid will suffer their own stump-steady karma amid resilient sprays of bamboo washed with storm. Meanwhile, I splash ink from the brush, stretch the borders of the page to contain the shifting zodiac over hills and rivers. I commit myself to this blank page, just as I'd like to commit to each arriving moment within the day. Nothing's certain, yet from all that's uncertain or lost in the leaf-strewn corners of what we do not understand, arrives a shine, a whistling gale, a jagged beam more intense than looking into the sun. This shine is the emptiness of infinity where everything's okay, the essential tranquillity where the artist's secret vision breaks from its wily seed and gives new shape to the world. Heavy with importance, light as a raindrop, this arrival is our feast, our temporary home, our galaxy of the moment, our bold, distant possibility brought near.

What happened when we walked from Angkor Wat's sanctuaries of stone goddesses at play in their green garden sauna, was that out mutual eye regained Delight, the essential drink of immortality, the Amrita par-excellence of our true nature. I felt gratitude in the thick heat under celestial faces winking from carved lintels—for the breath of the Muse that steadies or alarms us, sails us onto the open horizon, walks us though the tangled path, ears blazing with the ring of invisible spheres. And gratitude, too, among the faces of Cambodian families spreading food on mats under gold-wrapped trees. One evening, there above us all in that human drink of elephantine loneliness, I again caught glimpse of that purple-toweled monk we saw on our first evening, climbing Phnom Bakheng. He was levitating in flowing saffron, his smile even wider than before, as if, in his essential baldness, he knew all along that the ache of third-eye strain that the world's mistaken kings have created in their must-have doom spelled GREED would be relieved by Angkor Wat: its stone benches empty and wet, its shimmering dance of fiery tiaras and floating spires waiting for travelers like us—the us that is not separate from others, "not higher, not lower, no stages and no definite attainments, no mysterious stigmata or secret holyhood, no wild dark knowledge and no venerable authoritativeness." (Jack Kerouac: *The Scripture of the Golden Eternity*)

## 6 NOVEMBER: PHNOM PENH

A blooming bougainvillea draped over a teakwood house open to the streets, its windows without glass, framed with thin timber. Thus, no reflections. You don't see yourself when you look in. Instead, you meet people. A back room is for rent; we take it. Futon, white cotton sheets, louvered window facing the next door house, from which comes the banter of children playing. The ringing cyclos and dusty streets don't reach us here. But a waft of cooking does: cloves, ginger, coriander, basil, curry from the café below.

I'm remembering Moritz Thomsen today—I suppose because we're eating soup and baguettes, there's classical music in filtered sunlight, the joy of camaraderie. Every writer should have a writer like Moritz in his or her life: a maverick with cockiness, discipline, wit, savvy who works with the hands, lives humbly, enjoys music, makes space to write, has time for others. "One whose life and work validates your own," as Renée puts it. Moritz, the old man of 48 when I was 23, was the first to say, "balance the writer's life with another trade"—carpentry, social work, nursing, commercial fishing. He critiqued my writing under his plastic eyeshade, between a bottle of red wine and a hatchet. He always had a new book to recommend. He smiled at my travels on the cheap, probably because they resembled his own.

Moritz was sweltering on the Ecuadorian coast; I was freezing my ass off among Andean volcanoes. We were Peace Corps volunteers, keeping strange hours over portable typewriters after the day's work. We often met for French onion soup and baguettes in a Quito bistro. The waiter played Mozart on an old phonograph. We'd order wine, break bread, begin our ramblings. In one of his books, Moritz sized up a conversation: "Part of the middle-class tragedy lies in the facility with which intense experiences can be bought." Too many people were simply fleeing one life for a temporary other, he said, and in the process of touring (but not really visiting) places, were helping destroy them. Moritz eventually bought land, lived many years in Ecuador, wrote three memorable books: *Living Poor, The Farm on the River of Emeralds, The Saddest Pleasure.*

Thirty-five years later, Moritz is gone, Quito is a destination spot. Cambodia, too, opens itself full-out to the world's fastest growing industry: tourism. No matter the languages I speak, how cheaply I travel, how down-home I lodge, I'm part of it. Even if I go to Mongolia, stay for awhile, and shit in a hole, I'm hooked into the industry. Call myself traveler rather than tourist, seeker rather than traveler, so what? I'm the same old foreigner to the visa man, customs official, cyclo driver, food vendor, red-light girl, monk, charity worker, guide, innkeeper, pancake lady, shoeshine kid—all who want my money, however much, whatever little. I'm a walking dollar sign. Moritz was too, though in those days tourism wasn't big; you could easily disappear into the crowd. Besides, he was a South American resident, and when he finally left for Brazil one day, he traveled like a wandering bard, casting off the smug self-absorption of a middle class obsessed with buying, upgrading, filling life with material goods. He wanted nothing to do with the sludge of the upper class; he wanted to be nimble among the campesino, farmer, fisherman. In so doing, he confronted the inevitable wackery of the caste system, the awful capacity of a man to mock another man, and the brilliant resilience of poets and revolutionaries to mock dictators and corporations with songs of resistance.

On that memorable Brazilian venture, Moritz had only an extra set of clothes in a busted Pan Am flight bag, big enough for a football. But he also had his round-trip air ticket, travelers' checks, and medicine.

With cane sap spotting his trousers and mud on his shoes, he was suddenly off the farm, a tourist! Once he told me, "With a set of clothes, and a set of values, too, you'll spend more in a day than the locals will see in a year." True. With lightning speed you help transform the place you visit into your own. You came to stay in a house on stilts? It's now a concrete hotel with elevators, owned by an ex-Khmer Rouge captain. The townsfolk who grew up without anything? They suddenly need it all—but can't afford it. It's priced for the tourist, whose dollars stay at the top, barely reaching the cook or sweeper. Soon the locals hate their place, and begin their exodus. Moritz, three decades ago:

"Everything is going
and all for nothing."

Sun already hot, 9 A.M. Too distracted to work in journal. Writing is a cramped exercise. Big question mark naked under the mosquito gauze. A smile that forgets as soon as it turns the corner. A dimple that wants more. A broken back that remembers. I swat a fly, miss, hit the bougainvillea. I look down at my lap; its shaded balls and dreaming cock are foreign to me. So is the cat jumping from window to tin roof. So's my pencil. It has two points. One writes the sumptuous orchid with soft yellow labia; the other, the haze around that human rag of a man sawing ice on the curb. Voices gossip, stir the air. Someone hammers, someone sneezes, someone's on a toilet, sick. I feel dizzy enough to write a poem. —Malaria?

We leave our notes and have coffee with the 18-year-old human relief worker, who lives downstairs. She tells us she came to Cambodia from the U.K. "because I just couldn't sit in front of the TV any longer and watch the world. I had to participate in it." In *Return to the Source*, the seeker Lanza del Vasto goes to India, lives with Gandhi, and reminds us:

> "touch and feel
>   through action, bow to all
>   by stooping to work."

We've met ex-pats along the way, but they talk more about where they're from than where they are. Peace Corps workers are still around, humbled by new language and culture, usually an honest balance between what they take and what they give. I was one once, the greatest awakening of my life. But I got much more than I gave. Likely it was a great load off the locals when my time was up. They had enough to be responsible for in their own lives, let alone the kid from America who could hardly boil water. Speaking of Peace Corps, yesterday I had the fortune of celebrating my 60th with not only my beloved, but with a dear old buddy who I slogged through the upper Amazon with: Jeff Ashe. His trip to Cambodia synchronized with ours. He's here with Oxfam; still involved in social change, humane work on an understandable scale. An accomplished photographer, his portraits of rural peoples from Asia and Africa are exquisite, as are his close-ups of Angkor's majestic shrines and carved thresholds.

We have beers, then cruise the streets to the Royal Palace. Late sun on the auspicious convergence of the Tonle Sap and Mekong, a wide riverscape fronted by a lovely promenade where we mix with families, alms seekers, an elephant stoically walking Sisowath Quay with its master, the bird and insect eaters, the jello and egg vendors, flower ladies, mats of fortune tellers and scribes, monks in saffron, little girls with scales (your weight for 4¢), palm readers, coconut carvers, and street sweepers with bandit-like scarves covering their faces. Jeff looks fine, spacy as ever, tall and slumped as he always was, in that position of eternal giving— to those at the bottom, not the top, thus rocking the entire pyramid. Under his Nepalese baseball cap, his eyes twinkle with bemusement, eternal size up. He's going to organize, get things done. Watch the tree grow, the human fruit ripen.

Dragon fruit and mangosteen. Stir-fried beetles piled into fast-food pyramids on newsprint. Girl on bicycle in bronze sunlight, royal blue pajamas and red hat. Gray elephant, a cardboard cut-out in its own dust, poops on the promenade. Fish vendor bends over a cart, hands us a menu: GRILLED THE PRAWN—SOUP THE SQUID—FRIED THE VEGETABLES. We walk to the Foreign Correspondents Club, upstairs into classic, French-colonial, yesteryear hangout. Balconies overlook the river with its wildly lit decorations for bonn-om-tuk, the water festival. Big ceiling fans, big leather chairs, a wooden bar that goes on and on. Friendly Khmer girls wander the Naples-yellow room with trays of cold beer. "But where are the correspondents?" Renée asks. Maybe that's one, or that's one, I laugh. But they are probably CIA.

More beers, then to a quiet, surreal restaurant, furniture piled downstairs, big clock ticking near the door. Jeff treats us to mint-onion-lime spicy shrimp salad, basil-beef curry, and seafood satay. The waiters have smiles and dirty sleeves; they bring candles, disappear into the shadows. The dining room opens to a balcony overlooking a row of ragged rickshaws parked between moonlit frangipanis, as if in a sinister Shanghai 1936 movie. What a wonderful meal; what a strangely perfect place to say goodbye:

> in the kitchen
> fish playing in cold water
> under the butcher block.

## 7 NOVEMBER: PHNOM PENH

Renée and I watch a documentary at the Genocide Museum. In it a surviving grandmother talks about the Khmer Rouge: "I can understand love. But I cannot understand this. I cannot understand how it happened. I just cannot understand. That is why I cannot talk about it."

I still like to believe, as I did in Ecuador, as I do as a poet, that all of us—deep down in the psychic waters—speak the same lingo; that we have need for each other; that love, active compassion, is the key that fits all locks. But—so much hate and brutality in the world! Live long enough, watch the human wheel wobble a little more. One day it'll drop off its axle for good. Our neighborhood in Phnom Penh has a landmark: Toul Sleng, the Genocide Museum. In the 1970s it was a two-story concrete high school that the Khmer Rouge turned into "S-21"—torture chamber and death row for thousands of men, women, and children, Cambodians and foreigners alike.

To see the now-made-public photos the KR took of those they chained, shackled, whipped, beat, hung upside down, traumatized with electric rods, raped, clubbed, burned, starved, and shot, is to wake into the dream of impossibility. Some of the captives are defiant, some hopeful, some crazed with despair. All have been brutalized beyond what we can imagine. Do we all speak the same lingo; do we have need for each other?

> from a house facing
> the death camp
> a mother's lullaby.

The cleaning girl enters our room to place orchids, pale purple, in a tiny vase. She is slight, older than she looks. Her skin gives off a rained-on scent. She does the heavy work with long arms, graceful back, slender waist, extended fingers. She brushes the floor, goes about arranging the futon. Her bare brown feet are those of the dancer carved in sandstone at Banteay Srei. She never looks up so I don't know her eyes. Uncomfortably, she speaks a little English. Inches from me, her life moves by as if on a faraway horizon. Outside, clinking leaves, drift of trash smoke, crow caw, slap-thud of someone doing laundry, a whip-like sound. The girl leaves, her scent stays. I see my face in the mirror, and reject it. The smile, the shiny too-big-of-a-thing under the red eyes called the nose. The wrinkles, pockmarks. The dry, thinning hair on head; hair in nostrils and ears. Moritz's wrinkled map of a face, which I admired and feared then, is nothing compared to this. Not my face, couldn't be!

A boy walks to school whistling through a hibiscus leaf. Next door, a priest chants Sanskrit on the radio. Downstairs they play Mozart, as if the ghost of Moritz had summoned the waiter to put him on. We pack to leave, everything in two reasonable backpacks. I flip through spiral notepad, review scribbles, find Angkor Wat drawings and splices of conversations with our guide, Ponheary:

"Pardon is the way
of the warrior."

Perhaps I have crossed the ocean simply to hear Ponheary's amid-the-ruins discourse. Maybe there is nothing more to the trip than what I least expected: to witness her non-engagement in anger or grudge, in contrast with the furious, gun-pointing ones who fill the news back home. In the face of Ponheary's courage, our rulers lack courage. Courage to overcome their own fear, to renounce violence. Easier to be angry, hold grudges, invent a war, prioritize the combat game, take pleasure in the attack. Before leaving New Mexico, we heard Arundhati Roy speak: "Our strategy should be not only to confront the empire, but to shame it—with our art, music, literature, our joy, brilliance, relentlessness. Let's tell our own stories, ones different from those we're being brainwashed to believe."

Rue Pasteur. A Sri Lankan dive: masala dosa, flatbread, lassies. Beggars arrive, legless, like those on the Tonle Sap pier as we ferried out of Siem Reap for Phnom Penh. Aboard the boat, tourists aimed cameras at the extended families jammed into shanties; naked boys by their empty crab traps; naked girls in doorless huts built from rusty beer signs and flattened cooking-oil tins. Some on the boat tossed candies and band aids, waving and smiling. The kids didn't smile; they ran furiously for the goods, the big ones overpowering the small. They fought, hoarded, cried. The ferry moved on. For many aboard, because we were gone, the poverty was gone too:

> in the haze
> sky and water
> become one.

I want tranquillity to be the pervasive memory, not despair. But those families, in the heat of the harbor, crammed into their shanties, are still there. They stay, we go. After the war, they lost everything, becoming instantly homeless, set adrift by those who's nature it was, and is, to destroy. How many times have we seen the world work this way before: the power-elite stepping up their greed, their craving for things to go their way, their need to pull what they can into the kingdom of the rich?

Yesterday, at the National Museum, I realized I had crossed the ocean for another reason. Renée and I were taking a break from the exhibits, sitting on a bench in the outside courtyard, a quiet area of trimmed hedges and rectangular walkways within the museum walls. Without warning, a line of monks in bright orange robes filed into the patio. Hitting a shaft of late-afternoon sun, they burst into flame—and halted. One wanted to take a photo. He assembled the others in front of a statue in the middle of a pool, then waved me over. —Me? "Yes, yes. Please join group." Suddenly I found myself bathed in a bright orange sea of smiles. The monk put the camera to his eye, snapped the shutter. After a quick group bow, they were gone: into the darkness of the gallery in the next wing, the one with the naked devas.

Renée came to my side. We both looked at the pool where I had posed with the monks. The statue was Yama, god of the underworld. Around him we noticed four tiny bouquets of jasmine tied with smoking incense, a bouquet for each cardinal direction. At his feet, under the water, spelled out with smooth pebbles:

> IF YOU WANT A GOOD REBIRTH
> YOU MUST LIBERATE FROM
> THE DELUSIONS.

YangShuo, Guangxi CHINA:

I want to Live a Life of Laquered RED, with BURSTS of GOLD FOIL ON Micaceous STONE, Die The COLOR of fLowing TURQUOISE, Be BURIED iN MARIGOLD with RIBBONS of INDIGO, COLD WATER guRGLING THROUGH DRY UMBER LAND.

# CHINA:

## YUNNAN, GUIZHOU, GUANGXI

*Nobody understands why we do what we do*
*this cup of sake does*
IKKYU
(1450)

## 11 NOVEMBER 2003: BANGKOK

We rise early at the Bamboo Guest House, a nice find off the Chao Phraya via a small bridge over Klong Banglamphu into a neighborhood along the canal with a Buddhist wat, ice factory, street eateries, and some traditional teak houses—not many neighborhoods like this left in Bangkok. Our upstairs room faces wood balconies brightened with potted flowers, drying laundry, caged songbirds. Downstairs: communal showers, modest dining area, orchids blooming in freshly watered baskets, the manager's desk with *Bangkok Post*, crookneck lamp, antique fan, spindle of room tabs.

Unusually cool breeze today. Women already on the sois, fanning clay braziers, setting tables with coffee and rice porridge, chopping lemon grass and mint, heating rice noodles. Neighbors run back and forth, half dressed, sharing street and teak. The soi is simply another room of the house. Spices fill the air. Steam wafts from cooking vats. Factory workers tie on aprons, holler, joke, load trishaws with huge blocks of ice. Saffron-robed monks file house to house, extending lacquered alms bowls. Then, slap slap, barefoot, back to their gilded wat filled with bodhisattva icons under sweeping eaves, each tipped with a flaming spiral and chiming wind bell. Towering above:

> a cremation chimney
> its blackened vents
> circled by white doves.

Let me take leave of the world on a morning like this! Jasmine on the breeze, *wheee* of the ferryman's whistle, scuffle of schoolgirls in orchid uniforms, grandma sprinkling bromeliads with an oversize watering can, calico kitten undoing the thread from a tailor's sewing machine. Bangkok's notorious traffic gears up, but largely behind the barrio's action: twittering birds, a cook chopping cabbage, a woman washing a tray of translucent pink squid, a vendor sorting clay votive tablets in a cardboard box. The world hasn't quite happened. Into its dream of completion I wake, find a clean shirt, flatten wrinkles, curse an ink spot, go to the sink, brush teeth. Korean girl on my right does the same. Amsterdam man on my left, ditto. In the window, thin moon, purple sky. Three weeks into a two-month journey and my one-pair-of-two socks already has a hole in the big toe.

Pablo Neruda, who lived in Asia as a diplomat, said the sacred duty of the poet is "to leave and return." So it is I open the gate, walk off the path into the world's sideshow, lose control, flutter back into shape with a shift of perspective. I try to behave myself in the relentless warp and weft of humanity, sea breaking against island, glaciers retreating into stars, mice working under floorboards; but I'm unable to play it straight. All these nerve endings roused with unexpected sensation! Delight in chance, unpredictable encounters, direct meaning of things. Participation, separation. Dance of home life again, psyche aslant, mind loose. That's one element of the journey. Another's the urge to sit still, write, reel in what was missed while all was happening. The paradox, to quote Neruda: "When I am writing, I'm far away; and when I've come back, I've gone."

## 12 NOVEMBER: BANGKOK TO KUNMING

Thai Air circles out of Bangkok over low shacks, gleaming temples, slick highrise, bobbing ferries, flat-bottom barges tracing furrows in the Chao Phraya. I spot the ungainly banner, WELCOME ALL APEC DELEGATES, strategically stretched across riverfront shanties to hide them from a convention of Asia-Pacific Economic Delegation members (including George Bush). An hour north, over Chang Mai, we're served fish and noodles washed down with wine, followed by a shot of cognac. Lowering into Yunnan, jet engines whine over wooded slopes, hacked-away cliffs, quarries, smoking kilns, low brick suburbs blending into high concrete towers of downtown Kunming.

The Camellia Hotel, a traveler's favorite. Each room priced at Y 120 (approximately 8 yuan = 1 U.S. dollar) has a dependable shower, hot water thermos, complimentary green tea, wood comb, toothbrush, paper bedroom slippers. No heat, but the beds have thick cotton comforters. If it was warm, we'd relax in the two chairs overlooking the camellia garden below. Winter, though, nary a blossom. In the lobby, a bilingual staff of young women changes our money, issues our breakfast tickets, and helps us purchase train tickets for the 12-hour ride into Guizhou Province. We'll travel with friends Jacquie and Steve on part of this leg; in Guiyang join a university student who will guide us into the remote areas of Guizhou to visit Miao (Hmong) and Dong (Kam) villages.

We shower, head to the first floor, examine local teas, antique coins, jade bowls ("Fable Old Bowl Made of Nature Bring Blessedness to Who Possess It"). We walk the streets, find the flower market, inspect orchids, miniature pines, songbirds, goldfish, porcelain dragons, inks, chops, bamboo pens, and hand-painted "minority people" dolls. We try Kunming's specialty, Crossing-the-Bridge Noodles, but aren't impressed. Renée buys a jade bracelet; Jacquie a calligraphy brush. I get a new winter hat, baked sweet potato, wool socks, and stamps.

> writing postcards
> no mother
> no father.

## 14 NOVEMBER: KUNMING

Renée dreams of Angkor Wat Buddhas, walls of them. When she chants, her breath causes the reliefs to swell. "I must be tapping into an earlier life!" Over breakfast of steamed vegetables, noodles, fruit, and Yunnan coffee, she looks exquisite in her palette of deep purple, burnt orange, moss and sepia. Behind her: gold calligraphy of swimming carp in the lobby aquarium. Glass doors open to the city's even-tempered bustle of bicycles, buses, pedestrians. The two porters by the doors are dressed in ridiculous uniforms pinned with tin badges of earthly rank— a fitting metaphor for China's bureaucracy. It is they who impersonally open the doors to the country or close them for whatever reason, political or personal. Tomorrow we'll leave Kunming for Guiyang, all day and into the evening, northeast on the Wuhan Express. As the land unrolls, hopefully we can relax and update our journals. Oscar Wilde: "I never travel without my diary. One should always have something sensational to read on the train."

Yesterday, hiking Xi Shan, the Western Hills, we came across a sign in one of the cliff shrines: GREAT TALENT IS REVEALED BY ARDUOUS WORK. The physical act of in situ jotting is part of the work. So is backing away from the experience to let random impressions, third-eye takes, unfocused images sift through the psychic strainer. Phil Whalen said "My writing is a picture of the mind moving." Leaving home, abandoning the usual routine, cleans the pores. Clodhopping, bumping along by bus, savoring a train's steady rhythm shakes loose the head, lets in spontaneous flash of raw music, what Ferlinghetti called *Pictures of the Gone World*. After the scribbles, the winnowing begins. Seed chaff flies, essential kernels remain. Between idea of travel and reality of travel exists a strange world. The journal reveals it.

## 15 NOVEMBER: GUIZHOU PROVINCE

If a Han city or town was written up with praise in a guide book five years ago, forget it. It's now rubble, quickly being torn up and remade block-concrete new. Why? Because of tourists like us, and scores of traipsing Chinese led by doll-faced girls waving yellow pennants, chattering through cardboard megaphones. The poorest provinces are betting on tourism, failing to realize that what they are tearing down is what tourists have come to see. Kunming's old quarters—the low, grassy-tiled brick houses with round entranceways, clay walls curved like a dragon's back around stone courtyards—have all disappeared. Only two worthy streets and the Muslim quarter remain. Amid the new towers there's even a Wal-Mart, that predatory capitalist enterprise whose $250-

billion annual sales is greater than the economies of all but 30 of the world's nations.

Several good things about Kunming, though: the traveler scene is congenial; food is excellent; there's a university; cafes with real coffee; green belts to cool off in; bookstores with silk-bound volumes of poetry, history, architecture, and art. The Western Hills are close, with ancient temples amid flowering deciduous. The whole city is available on an easy, double-decker bus system, including a park where old-timers fly kites and young stroll arm in arm by a placid lake (unheard of ten years ago). Of course, looking at photos of Kunming taken a decade ago, even five years ago, I realize I'm in the fast-forward of what it's become: straight-edged, conforming, out to please a surge of visitors who stay longer and spend more once they realize they've got the same amenities they've enjoyed on their last dozen package-tour stops. That they're out here at all, instead of in front of their televisions, is laudable. Yet, I often side with writer Philip Adams: "To many people holidays aren't voyages of discovery, but a ritual of reassurance." One can pay lots of money, travel far, yet easily remain aloof from the world—viewing it through a cocktail glass or video camera, cocking the head to a cell phone or bending over a laptop.

Train rattles along. Chalky hills steepen. Egg man pokes his head into our berth, followed by grapefruit lady, milkmaid, noodle man. In the next compartment, a wild card game. Shuffles, slaps, laughter, howls. Cigarette smoke, not ink-brushed mist, gives character to the passing landscape. Haze envelopes the window as we stand in the rocking aisle watching terraced fields, scraggly orchards, passing haystacks cling to hills. A farmer bundles wood, another goes at the hardpan with a metal bar. One sculpts a dirt levee; one struggles behind massive oxen. Between jagged boulders: tiny plots of mustard, cabbages, onions, collards. A half-erased sun spins from the pines over ragged barrancas, only to disappear into mottled air drifting in from the next valley, and the next.

We reflect on a stellar meal we enjoyed in Kunming. En route to the Western Hills we met a young man from Guangzhou, He Xiao Feng, who was visiting Kunming on business. Brilliant guy, proficient in English, versed in ancient and contemporary Chinese writers ("Bei Dao's work was more alive when he lived in China; not so interesting now"). We spent the afternoon together hiking endless steps to shrines and conversing. Afterwards we invited him for dinner, to Mama Fu's, near the Camellia. Once seated he scanned the menu, looked around, and quickly sized things up. "This is where Chinese come to try Western Food. May I suggest a place where we can sample Yunnan food? It comes highly recommended."

We bolted, grabbed a taxi into the narrow streets of old Kunming—and lo!—found ourselves entering the temple-like structure that caught our attention the day before: a dark-paneled house with antique dining rooms surrounding an open-air courtyard. On the walls, ornately carved wooden frames held polished slabs of round stone engraved with poetry. Dream stones! I had seen such "pictures" once, at the Metropolitan Museum of Art, in a reconstructed 12th-century Chinese scholar's residence. Extracted from marble quarries, the stones are sliced to reveal miniature landscapes in their veinings. They are said to be the breath-force of mountains.

We were shown to a courtyard table. Behind us open doors and lattice windows revealed rowdy groups eating meals with great gusto around glass turntables laden with pork, noodles, bean curd, frog legs, fungus, and water chestnuts (loud slurps, sucks, and ecstatic cries of delight, while to the floor went beer bottles, napkin wads, bones, and snail shells). Immediately a host of waitresses surrounded us to pour green tea, all wearing wax-resist indigo tunics with red frogs up their sides. After topping our cups with a second round, they stood back waiting for orders. He Xiao was pleased. It was the right place for his guests. He asked for the menu, and inquired in a serious tone about the recommended Yunnanese specialties.

Bubbly, locally brewed beer arrived. We toasted, and he meticulously placed the order. First came an entree described as: "seven-mushroom powder plus local chook," a chicken broth to which we added spoonfuls of rich forest-tasting dried mushroom powder. "In China we eat everything. It must be fresh. This is medicine from the mountains, it will make you strong." Then followed: "pepper chili-garlic peanut-oil boletus"/"fried potherb birch flowers with pear"/"Yunnan goat cheese with red-chili dip" (mild, semi-cured cheese pressed into thin sheets and fried)/ "whole garlic lake fish" (sauteed amid crimson-gold peppers, midsection deboned, cut into cubes for easy plucking with chopsticks) /"steamed pork dumplings" (pot stickers)—and little dishes of pickled wild plants. For dessert: crisp Yunnan apples and shots of plum liquor. Easily the most memorable meal of a lifetime. Jacquie pointed out bonsai pines and camellias in porcelain urns around us. "Probably a thousand years old!" she laughed. Before leaving, we reviewed the menu again, jotting down a sampling of what we didn't try:

FLUENT BEAN FLOWER
SOFTEST HEART
100 YEARS BUCKLED MEAT
CHARACTERISTIC QUICK FRY RAW INTESTINE
TRUTHFUL DUCKFOOT
FRIED BEE CHRYSALIDES
RICHES AND HONOR OF GOLD SHRIMPS
COOKED PIGBRAINS IN CHINESE POT WITH SPRING SAUCE
GOOD TASTE OF YARDFLOWER IN LONG CHILI
SKEWERED INCENSE BULL FROG
SPECIAL FLAVOR OF GRASS CARP
SUPER BRAISED MEAT WITH GREASINESSLESS IN 100 YEARS
DECOCTED CAKE IN CREAM SAUCE
BEAN FLOWER CATTLE MEDULLA
CLOAKED CHOOK AND BEAN CURD WITH ODOR
OX LIVER MUSHROOM
SOUR FOOT TENDON
LOTUS LEAF PLUM BUCKLING MEAT
GOOD TASTE OF COCK

On the slopes out the train window are villages of the dead: tombs carved with Chinese characters, freshly weeded and fed. Down low are villages of the living: houses rising from paddies, changing color valley to valley, according to the earth they are made from: umber, yellow ochre, gray, Mars red. Rock and mud houses with tile rooftops dot the remote valleys; cement houses with satellite dishes crowd the towns. All goes by as we snack on roasted chestnuts, yogurt, and buns confiscated from this morning's hotel buffet.

                    the train passes . . .
                    farmers weeding
                    don't look up.


    I drift, doze, wake inside a hill temple outside Kunming. Gnarled pomegranate trees over raked paths. A custodian coughs inside a buttoned-up jacket, sets aside his wood-toothed rake, puts a cigarette to a pyre of leaves, watches smoke coil into the sky. I slip by unnoticed to the Terrace of Sleeping Dragons. A crude map on my entrance ticket indicates the Pavilion of Great Liberation is close by. I open a gate, find only forbidden paths, locked doors, dead-end alleys rank with urine. There's a wilted bouquet under a bucket of glaze, cracked immortals on a sawhorse. Lofty bamboo bends with musical sighs, lower stalks etched with Chinese. Unable to read them, I'm left to invent. Have the inscriptions been carved by lovers, monks, a dutiful gardener noting when he last fed his peonies?


                    old garden—
                    water music
                    from swaying bamboo.


    I hop an iron chain, climb a stairway. My eyes slide down glazed roof tiles into the hills. Odor of raw earth halts my vision. Slopes are torn of trees, a blade of smog slices the canyon. Progress bulldozes forward, gobbling magnolias and pine. My eyes retreat to the courtyard below. A smoking cauldron sends paper money to the ancestors. Pilgrims saunter away, past the Hall of Supreme Harmony, blowing snot to the freshly swept stone. No Pavilion of Great Liberation here. I peel ginger candy, leave the foil for crows. Green mist wraps a persimmon tree near a chamber where Avalokitesvara smiles above a frail, shaved-head figure seated in a plastic chair over an open book:

> between prayers
> the old nun
> lifts a cheek to fart.

An adjoining room reveals a pantheon of painted clay statues, dozens of sculpted weirdos who laugh, stare, float, mock with ludicrous eyes and thin, fasting bodies. Arhats. Mendicants. Seers. Sages. Bad boys. Monks. Madmen. A garish bearded meditator scowls at a monkey pulling his sleeve. A sharp-ribbed, fasting ascetic tears open his chest to reveal a miniature Buddha smiling under his heart. A hermit with a conspicuous bulge in his robes leans lustfully over a woman with flushed cheeks and generous hips. She is about to massage his feet, but her eyes are elsewhere. The creator of this unlikely pantheon was Li Guangxiu, who, in the 19th century, spent 10 years at the task, only to be banished, his creations too far out for his patron.

I ditch my quest for the Pavilion of Great Liberation. The repetitive courtyards, perfect alignments, overstated gardens are too strict for my taste. Always the raised terraces to evoke mythic mountains; the ponds to symbolize sacred oceans; the predictable arched bridge over water lilies; the stray peach blossom drifting, according to plan, into the Scholar's Garden to rest among patterned stone, trimmed hedges, trellised benches intended for contemplation. Offsetting this perfection is a quaint wooden shrine where an overweight figure sits with a worried smile:

> Buddha of the Future
> his altar decorated
> with termite holes.

I investigate a rear temple in disrepair. Plaster has fallen from the walls to reveal baked adobes, smoky gold. No Buddhas here, no ancestors, no gods of luck, no Avalokitesvara, or farting nun. Only pollen rising from my heels in minute electrical charges. On the way out I sidetrack through the Green Chamber. Frescoed walls, painted ceilings, hand-hewn cabinets strong with musk. Wisteria flowers drape latticed windows (I know behind them someone watches); filigree shadows dance about the floor. Lingering here, I contemplate sex, death, the possibility of rebirth. Maybe I'll return as the praying mantis the boy on the balcony has trained on a string. As for the Pavilion of Great Liberation, it's okay that I didn't find it. Site #7 on the map is perhaps a more appropriate place for me to linger: The Wall of Temporary Progress. It's near the entrance gate, where my friends are waiting, eating roasted yams. A good, simple taste under the perfect blue sky. We hire a taxi to Kunming. Through the windshield, a figure at work in tangled branches:

> old monk pruning plums
> the thin arms
> of my father.

## 15 NOVEMBER: ARRIVAL IN GUIYANG

"Gone With the Wind" plays from the ceiling speakers of the Wuhan Express. Renée returns from the WC, alarmed. The enormous stainless steel toilet rising from the wet floor is unapproachable, seatless, designed for giants. Its deep-down bowl is jammed with a snake nest of turds. Outside the toilet, men crouch low in the aisle, pressing tobacco into their pipes. Guizhou backcountry passes. Brown canyons, harvested paddies, stony soil. Sharp slopes in silvery mist. After many tunnels, bridges, and an unbelievably ugly steel-mill city flaring and sputtering amid open seams of coal, night falls. We arrive at Guiyang ("precious sun"), meet Liao Jing Lin, our guide, in a crowd of gawkers. She quickly ushers us into a waiting cab to our hotel. Tomorrow, first thing, we'll head to Kaili by bus, three hours into eastern Guizhou, to visit Dong, Miao (Hmong), and Gejia villages.


## 16 NOVEMBER: KAILI

I'd hoped for a frontier town with dirt streets, but Kaili is the predictable jumble of newly finished monstrosities. There's a snazzy downtown, but the rest is a jumble of half-built streets, open sewers, crushed shanties, in-progress hotels. Dust rises from the overkill of sweepers whisking streets, but leaving public restrooms untouched. Our hotel is up a lane where vendors sell tangerines and apples, sweet and succulent. Our room is clean and cheap, Y70, private bath. We've learned enough Chinese to get the staff to turn on the hot water and heat. We shower and do laundry. Downstairs, over the unstaffed desk, are three clocks. One shows Guizhou time; another Beijing time; the third, labeled "Lon Don," is broken. On the desk, a block of wood engraved with English letters, reads: INJORATION. I point this out to our guide, who unsmilingly gives a shrug. Behind the desk is another sign:

> FOR YOUR SAFTEY
> PLEASE KEEP CASH VALUABLES
> IN HEAD STAGE.

Outside is an eatery popular with locals. We want to try it, but Liao Jing is worried. "You want to eat in *there*?" Yes! She bends to our wishes with a bit of hidden delight. As a student, she's been instructed to care for these "important Americans," an unreal responsibility that dampens the nature of our easygoing selves. Overly cautious, obsessed with our health, safety, and that we receive only good impressions of China, it's daunting to be around her. In addition, our days are suddenly scheduled with the kind of rigor that disallows unpredictable turns. It's a 180 swing from the way Renée and I love to travel, linger, get lost. But Liao Jing's good will and stamina are admirable. Without her, the ordeal of travel and lodging would be difficult, not to mention the language barrier.

The couple who runs the eatery is cheerful, eager to please, honored that we've chosen to sample their hotpot, to sit as the locals do: on low benches around a circular table where a propane-fired wok boils with water, chile paste, cooking oil. We're served the usual complimentary green tea, then order beer with plates of ultra-fresh greens, eggplant, tofu, seaweed, and mushrooms. Followed by fish, chicken, and battered pork. Using chopsticks, each person chooses a morsel, adds it to the boiling broth, and when done lifts it into a bowl of rice. I sample tofu and veggies. Absolutely delicious, especially with the fiery chile: a thick, smoky paste of ginger, garlic, roasted cayenne, and soybean oil.

Across the way, bearded elders dressed in dark blues hunker on low stools, puffing bamboo-stem pipes with glazed pottery bowls. Hmong women pass by, babies on backs in elaborately embroidered cloth carriers. After the meal, we follow them to a market filling a dusty avenue where more women, their hobo sticks tied with bundles, examine articles of tin, straw, aluminum, cast iron, and plastic. There's a fruit section, then the roosters, hens, dogs, ducks, geese, live piglets—all waiting to be sold in woven bamboo cages. We gesture with a little Mandarin and sign language, don't understand the reply, but enjoy the good cheer it produces. A medicine man sits over pulverized antlers, crushed bugs, ground sea creatures, pickled newts, mind elixirs, tumor reducers, virility boosters, cough syrup, erection raisers, and corked vipers in bottled blue liquid. I buy a two-cent whisk broom, receive my change in worthless, barely discernible, wrinkled paper bills.

A pair of Brueghal-like farmers passes, bent under smooth bamboo shoulder poles. They smoke and chatter vigorously. One carries half a skinned dog on the hook at the end of his pole, the tail half. The other carries the head half. Nearby, a woman sells winnowing baskets. An intoxicated man stops, picks one up, tries it on as a hat, begins to sing a folk tune, arms dangling in a puppet dance. The annoyed vendor coaxes him away. He moves to the knife section, grabs a pair of machetes, begins fencing, aiming the flashing blades at passersby. We decide it's time to move on.

The air is gray and drizzly, our least favorite climate. Sun, salt, dry air, herb-scented hills are deep in our blood. The better half of my family is from Napoli, Renée's from Calabria. Gray weather is not part of us, and here we are in a province where the saying goes: "without three li of flat land, three days of fine weather, three cents to rub together." Along Beijing Donglu we stop at a bakery for pastries and soy drink. I purchase a bottle of cheap sorghum wine, but it's so bad I leave it on a carpenter's motorbike as he bangs away in a shop. We return to our hotel to read. Tomorrow we'll visit Xijiang, a large Hmong village four hours in the hills south of Kaili.

## 17 NOVEMBER: KAILI

Wake to loudspeakers crackling martial arts music. Everyone up early, rigidly exercising in that dutiful way. Give me old-time gospel tambourines in Memphis, Los Jubilados tuning up in Santiago de Cuba, monks spinning prayer wheels in Tengpoche! Nothing obligatory dictated by state. But who here would oppose? Fear of voicing opinion, breaking the norm. So much history of "conform or be singled out for punishment" amid the ideology to make powerful the communal whole. Do I sense the ghost of Confucius waving the wand of proper behavior? Build character! Melt into the masses! Don't investigate your individuality!

> to blaring marches
> a row of gray pigeons
> nods on the powerline.

Singing for the "motherland" is a suspect way to begin the day (I'd rather sing for personal pleasure). But, then, there are plenty of American classrooms where saluting the flag and chanting the pledge is mandatory—often followed by televised "news," sponsored by you know who. Here, there, a leader gains control by distracting the masses, misinforming them, transforming them into joyless machines—tamed, muzzled, ready to serve the administration. The president doesn't answer to the people, or to experienced diplomats or respected world leaders. Suggestions contrary to official policy are regarded as suspicious, even unpatriotic. Questions aren't meant to be heard; they are meant to be dismissed. Under such circumstances, one's natural ability to care is ultimately suffocated, even turned into an unnatural ability to hate.

We dress and return to the bakery on Beijing Donglu for millet gruel, instant coffee, sweet rolls. Excitedly, we're off to catch our bus, but first Jacquie wants to buy one of those plastic, screw-lid tea jars that Chinese travelers are never without. At any bus stop you refresh it with hot water and your tea leaves last all day. Leaving Kaili we pass a mountainside being chewed up by chisels, bars, adzes. Hard labor of human muscle tearing into cliffs, hauling rock to conveyors to be reduced to sand and gravel, then into molds to be cast into cement beams to be delivered to construction sites where billboards announce "New Look For Our Progressive Motherland." (Liao Jing says her university will soon be moved to a new site, the old buildings leveled for housing to accommodate the influx of migrants from the countryside.) Along with the rock miners are a caste of workers who struggle with ropes to lift enormous chunks of coal onto metal scales to be weighed and sold.

Amid dust and glistening coal heaps inside a fenced premises, the workers make their homes: tin-faced shanties carved into pillaged cliffs, choking with hearth fumes. The Great Leap Forward continues! Daily, millions plod through work routines under the whip of the politically ambitious. Sick, sweating, and psychologically askew, these workers are still fulfilling quotas—even though the dictator has long since passed away.

In an hour the first Hmong villages appear from thickly wooded hills rising above patchwork river bottoms. In contrast to ugly, sprawling Han towns, these villages blend into the environment. Their multi-storied wooden houses are topped with tile roofs, a few of bark. Animals live in the first level, families upstairs. Gardens abound; fields glisten. Hay is wrapped around tall pines pruned of their lower branches. Renée loves them. "They look like pagodas!"

Hmong, according to a passage in Anne Fadiman's *The Spirit Catches You And You Fall Down*, means "the people," but in China they are called Miao: "barbarians, bumpkins, wild uncultivated grasses"—depending on who translates. During their 2000-year history of migrations from north of the Yellow River, they've continued into Laos, Vietnam, and Thailand. Over seven million Hmong live in China, half of them in Guizhou.

The bus bumps along, stopping often for Hmong families who accommodate themselves on plastic stools in the aisle as seats fill. Soon the bus is packed tight with lively song-like voices. Sentences bend upward with long, drawn-out endings. The women wear black velveteen blouse-jackets with silver, crimson, and turquoise-embroidered collars and cuffs. Plastic shoes, black trousers. Silver earrings and belts. Hair wrapped with yellow towels, or done into elaborate buns pinned with pink combs or silver barrettes. One woman bundles a hen in her lap. One, a child. Another carries a hunk of smoked meat on a tote stick. Another wedges a piglet between her feet. The men, some with goatees, wear dark blue trousers and jackets, fur headpieces or Mao-style caps. An old guy leans on a sweat-polished cane, smoking a pipe. Everybody's gossiping, trading jokes, falling into silence. Going to market in Xijiang!

> a distant river shines—
> that same blue light
> of her earrings.

Four hours of travel and the mountains close in, a covered bridge appears, the first of many "wind and rain bridges" Guizhou is noted for. It looks like a palanquin built on rails: pegged wood, tile roof, ornate fringe. Along the road every patch of tillable earth is planted with cabbage, mustard, and kale. The canyon narrows, my thoughts deepen. It's impressive, this phenomenon of so many Hmong people going *in*, to the back country, to trade among their own fellows in their own tongue, rather than *out*, into Han cities with their brash merchants and dirty streets. At one stop, I catch a schoolgirl's eye. We hold our gaze as she steps from a bamboo thicket. A cloud of dust, and she's gone. In the bus, a boy wedged between his elders in the aisle hardly looks at me. He's more interested in what he can see of the passing mountains—quite a contrast to the staring Chinese who check us out in buses and train stations with unabashed curiosity.

Vine-draped evergreens darken the slopes. Stone terraces zigzag up narrow peaks. Behind them, in woods and clearings, hundreds of villages must hide. We pass more of those curious haystacks, mirrored in ponds, and squat houses where potters fashion bowls in smoke-blackened doorways. On the train, vendors offer peanuts and oranges—and correct us when we mistakenly lay out yuan (locally known as kuai) instead of jiao. At one stop,

> a young peddler
> sells egg after egg
> from his ragged sleeve.

Around every turn we expect Xijiang. Then, when not looking, it's there—sprawling up and down the hills, smoke curling from post-and-beam houses. As we roll in past the rice paddies, a raucous group of women with bloody faces are huddled around someone. It seems they are both weeping and laughing at once. Liao Jing inquires and tells us: "They wear red dye when taking a bride from her parents to the house of her groom."

We pass a giant wooden trough where bolts of cotton are being stirred in indigo. A bit further, the food market: meat, sugarcane, eggs, tofu, star anise, red flower peppercorns, raspberries, pumpkins, loquats, persimmons, taro, bean shoots, and noodles. One vendor specializes in expensive bottles of Mao tai, offset by cheap crude liquor sold from plastic gas cans. We step over the pumpkin man's dried gourds to herb sellers quietly poised above ginger, lichen, jícama, coriander, red chile, ferns, and mushrooms. In the house and home section are assorted teakettles, hoes, picks, axes, handmade skirts, spools of ribbon, eyeglasses, cloth shoes, mirrors, make up, hardware, rope, fishing tackle, wooden canes, reed mats, funeral wreathes, firecrackers, plastic toys, and paper money for the dead. Throngs of buyers, nobody in a hurry, everybody ambling and looking with pleasure and exchange:

> market day
> the biggest knife
> on the prettiest woman.

Under a row of calendar girls pinned to a wire (seductive looks and hiked-up skirts as they board sleek, propellered airplanes) is an overstuffed couch, perhaps the ugliest piece of furniture we've ever seen: uneven eye-dizzying plaid designs, burnt orange and chocolate. Next to it is a stall filled with exquisite indigo batiks. They are made by Gejia women, their intricate geometric motifs drawn with molten beeswax on stone-rubbed cotton cloth. Some have a second application of lighter indigo to give the design a two-toned dimension. Renée purchases one for her writing room, $8. After perusing an assortment of silver jewelry, breastplates, earrings, tiaras, embroidered baby carriers, jackets, leggings and vests, we stop to examine pleated women's skirts. Some dazzle the eye with moiré sheens of greenish gold. Jacquie later learns it's pounded gentian that gives the color:

> returning my change
> the weaver's
> blue hands.

77

A hillside labyrinth of wooden houses overlooks the market. Ponies laden with cement, bamboo, sand, and charcoal plod continuously up the zigzag network of packed-earth trails. Women do the same, struggling under bags of grain slung on wooden poles. A man, hidden under a butchered hog, puffs heavily with each step. Someone suds laundry on stone; someone stirs indigo leaves into paste. Stilt houses on stone embankments are strung with chile and daikon drying under their eaves. In a doorway an upside-down basket serves as a mold over which a freshly starched and pleated skirt is drying. Some of these skirts, we are told, have over 500 pleats.

The last bus for Kaili leaves late afternoon, and we're soon hiking down the hills, back to market. On the return trip, a touching incident: a Hmong man standing in the packed aisle by my seat has said nothing to me on the ride down, but now turns and speaks in broken Mandarin as if I were an old friend. About to deboard in the middle of nowhere, he extends a lightly brushed handshake and disappears. "What did he say?" I ask Liao Jing. "Well, in bad Chinese he said to you 'I am going to say goodbye now. I have to get off here. I have a high mountain to climb.'"

Back in Kaili, exhausted, we opt for a meal at a vacuous restaurant where a group of Hmong villagers are gathered around a table, drinking, eating, carrying on with wild abandon. A chubby man stands, beats a chopstick against a glass; now everyone is up, singing in high voices that echo through the dining hall (we're the only other customers). Pure nadista indigenous brouhaha! Such abandon represents good manners in my book, but bad manners to the reserved culture of Liao Jing, who

78

gives a scolding wince. We laugh and acknowledge the celebration, much to her disapproval. I order rice wine, but what comes is Beijing sorghum; not quite what I had in mind, but it does the trick. We are famished and when the food arrives we dive in. Aubergine cooked with hot chile in peanut oil, sprinkled with ground pork and garlic. Broccoli in Guizhou sauce. Pot stickers with dipping sauce. A tasty plate of grilled tofu in sesame oil with red peppers and ground pork. All shared communally, washed down with the usual servings of green tea. About $1.50 each.

## 18 NOVEMBER: RONGJIANG

Awful town, torn up, getting ready—for what? Earthen walls, tiled roofs, cobbled alleys, sheltered markets, landscaped entranceways, all that is (was) traditional, now in a heap. It's challenging to walk; conduit and rebar pokes up everywhere, concrete tubes are rolled into open sewers. No one is working. Come next year, and the next, the town will likely still be under construction, the dream put off, everything sagging under abandoned scaffolding, money gone, the place bankrupt. The sweepers continue their task, though there aren't really any streets to sweep. A warm breeze stirs yellow dust into whirlwinds; we mask our faces with kerchiefs, looking like bandits dragging suitcases of questionable weight:

> in the wind
> a man without a hat
> holds his head.

79

The six-hour bus ride from Kaili and the many attempts to find lodging have drained us. We finally room at Rongjiang Binguan, a dump that's seen better days. No restaurant, but Liao Jing ingeniously borrows someone's kitchen and cooks us up a delicious pork-rice-mustard-greens and braised-tofu meal. We eat in our rooms amid musty, thick-curtained walls, maroon and midnight blue. Our bed sags; the bath has a broken tub, the water weak and brown; tiles are missing around the toilet, which flushes with a dangerous, gargling backlash. Despite the awfulness, or maybe because of it (no solace in the rude, unhelpful staff; none certainly in our shab-ass surroundings), Renée and I enjoy the best lovemaking on this leg of the trip. We roll out of it with teary-eyed laughter, afraid to fall on the carpet for fear of fungal infection. In the morning Renée relates a dream: "Old casa with coverings on the furniture. Layer of soot over everything. But I know if I work diligently to remove the dirt, I'll uncover the beauty."

Because the main road to Rongjiang was under repair, our bus took an interesting alternative route from Kaili, following the Duliu River. Even though the driver kept me anxious, speeding up instead of braking for the curves, I had time to hastily sketch many timeless scenes: slow-turning waterwheels nestled in terraced hills; jangling pony carts filled with peasants, hoes to the sky, wearing shiny, pounded-indigo cloaks; a child waving a twig behind an immense water buffalo; farmers plodding invisibly under giant bales of hay. Walking haystacks! The mountain air was thin blue, whitewater glinting behind the fields. Flat-bottomed boats, zen-like in the still mirror where the rapids calmed, were tied to limestone cliffs; willow branches swept the water; a gaggle of children dove and splashed.

I show my sketches to Renée, and she reads a passage from the Tao Te Ching: "The way of life means continuing. Continuing means traveling far. Traveling far means returning."

## 19 NOVEMBER: CONGJIANG

Easy three-hour ride along Duliu Jiang from Rongjiang. Classic river views from the bus: log jams, straw-shod rafts, a flash of flocking geese, cottages clustered in ficus trees under jade palisades. Here in Congjiang, a Dong village climbs the hill right behind us—pushed there because of the hotel, I suspect. We have a simple room, third floor, Y60: hot shower, comfortable bed, a lively balcony breeze to speed-dry our laundry. Hearth wood perfumes the air. We're lower down the valley, it's warm, and we're in much better spirits. I open an iced beer, relax, ruminate.

Why put up with this travail? Certainly there's need to experience a place firsthand; walk its topography; hear people's stories; know its myth, history, art, agriculture, politics, power—in situ. But there's also the inner sojourn. Dislodged from the norm, one unexpectedly discovers areas of the mind not so accessible at home. (Though one could argue that they *are* accessible there. You could harvest the peyote plant on the sill, smash habits created in familiar surrounds, drive without purpose, take to the outback, dislodge from emotional longings, the information web, the resurgent need to curse, shoplift, over-irrigate the trees, run off with the neighbor's wife.)

As much as I prefer the intimacy of weeding the basil and training primrose through rock crannies, I can't resist the lure of the far. It's a metaphor for the distance I want to go inside my mind. A few bumps in the road only replicate those of my father's sojourn in India, our family forays across the West, Great Uncle Zito's vaudeville travels. Add growing up in Southern Cal: finding balance on waves, rambling the desert until the needle hit empty, looking irresistibly west across the Pacific to the "East." Mix in post-war dreariness, suburban doldrums, Catholic nun dictators, obligatory draft, unjust war. And the equation equals Get Out! Smack your lips to Tempest Storm. Neck in the back seat to Hank Ballard. Roll to Ruth Brown. Jump the line into Mexico. Bust an axle in Baja. Join the Peace Corps. Drop into the Andes on a DC-3. Break a propeller in the Upper Amazon. Enter dream time on ayahuaska. Resist the draft, protest the war. Share ganja with third-eye rishis. Live in a shack, Ecuador. Live in a shack, India. Live in a shack, Sierra Nevada. Live in a shack, Sangre de Cristo. "Going too far," my father used to say. "But not far enough," I still say.

Maybe it's the simple pleasure of climbing the flanks of Annapurna for a solid look down into the madness of the loop. Or swimming a 120-meter drop off in the Bali Sea—just to know how frightening the abyss is and that it's possible to navigate it. Yep, size things up in buzzard crags. Test for an echo in rues, calles, cirques, cloisters, wats, icebergs, scree. See what I weigh in a hanging valley, a magnetic curve. Try a new language, get another head, sound my name on another continent. Talk to new people. Stumble through the empty quarter. Fly without lessons. Travail? Why not? Shake the ass, the cranium, the eyeballs, the entire belief system. Paddle outside the ropes, look around. Wander like an insomniac, seek the center of incandescence:

a crooked walking stick
keeps the path
straight.

Before leaving Rongjiang this morning we visited Chejiang, a Dong village 12 kilometers out of town on a river edged with lush fields. Met the owners of a crafts shop near a three-story drum tower. After much looking, we bought an embroidered cloth baby carrier decorated with silver trinkets, and a man's raincoat, the indigo cloth pounded to a high sheen, weatherproofed with egg white (adding animal blood gives the indigo an unusual reddish glow). All the while, hunkered in a back room, a 90-year-old grandma went about harvesting seed from a tangle of vines, glazed eyes, knotted hands precisely sorting each kernel into its rusty can.

Prior to exploring the town, we photographed the crafts-shop couple with their teenage daughter. She's been dressing in her absolute finest for a beauty contest/singing event about to commence on a stage in the village field. Her attire? A handmade indigo blouse embroidered with flowers and colorful geometric patterns up the sleeves and around the collar; a pleated miniskirt over indigo leggings tied with ribbons; a tiara of hand-worked silver horses, flowers, and conch-shaped pendants. Her ears are adorned with jade; her eyes accented with lilac mascara. Tying her waist is a wide belt of embossed silver jangling with pendants. Around her neck is looped a silver chain crafted of exquisite filigree. What a beauty!

Below the stage, husbands and wives crowd the field, dressed in identical finery. They look exquisite against the verdant hills. Some wear aprons bordered with stars, flowers, and teardrops around centerpieces of whirling spirals. Children play with hoops and plastic tops. The girls in embroidered blouses, indigo miniskirts, cotton leggings. Plastic flowers in hair. Hearts, amulets, silver chains around necks. We wander the crowd, hardly noticed. Everyone eyes the stage where performers take turns at microphones, some of the women singing a capella, others accompanied by men playing long-necked stringed instruments. Between rounds of applause, judges take notes. Jacquie giggles, noticing the women, perfectly poised on folding chairs and singing in harmony, are also at work embroidering geometric snowflakes on pairs of insoles—like those we bought in the crafts shop.

After a round of performances and judging (no Han influence here; this is entirely Dong), I stroll the riverside among weeping trees, cobble lanes, wooden carts parked upright against stone walls. Little ferry boats from another century, with rattan tops and painted railings, are tied to grassy moorings where ladies wash clothes and vegetables. Where the current bends under a banyan, I meet a pair of lovely young women, bright flowers in their hair, richly ornamented white blouses, black skirts and ribboned leggings, purple velveteen shoes. They're lingering on a bench, chatting in timeless serenity as I interrupt with a quiet bow. They respond cheerfully to this stranger's request for a photo, huddle together, and smile proudly with relaxed auras, right into the camera. I feel charged as we bid goodbye and I continue into narrow lanes, greeting people, savoring the architecture: pleated-bamboo fences, stone canals, a thatch gate, a granite step where sits a basket of freshly picked coriander. Its sweet, sharp pungency fills the air, while from afar, over gurgling water, comes the villagers' singing. Can I bear to leave this countryside? I am of leisure, but leisure is precious in these rippling hills.

music in the fields
pollen from sunflowers
where egrets fly.

Back at the performance area, I spy Renée at a portal leading into a courtyard where a private "girls show" is in progress: more of the same mini-skirt attire, only these late-teen beauties sport the shortest skirts of all, and entice the viewer by spinning lime-green paper parasols above their cerulean blouses and elaborate floral headpieces. They take turns doing a fashion walk with perfected turns, twists, hip swings, figure eights, and painted-finger mudras. Have they taken their cues from a Shanghai fashion channel? This is definitely a ladies-only event. A voyeur, I don't linger long. Instead, I return to the river, meander the banks, remember a haiku by Chiyo-ni, 18th century:

clear water
no front
no back.

As we leave Chejiang, a woman runs up, all smiles. It's the owner of the crafts shop, offering us a bag of tangerines for our departure. The goodwill on her beaming face—worth all the travail to get here.

## 20 NOVEMBER: CONGJIANG

*and she feeds you tea and oranges*
*that come all the way from China*
—Leonard Cohen

The warm air and succulent citrus of this part of Guizhou have my head light. Memories surge: of Mei, the painter from Fujian in my college art class, plucking a tangerine from a bowl on our first date, "the one with leaves, for good luck"; of Dalia, daughter of a Riobamba fruit vendor, tossing me a ripe tangerine through the train window on Easter Sunday; of the long-haired beauty at the Perfume Pagoda, piercing a green tangerine with her red nail; of sycamore leaves falling over a man napping on a tangerine cart, Kunming; of the tea lady offering, with both hands, Yunnan jasmine tea in a cup painted with tangerines:

> sampling tea
> know I've known
> her before.

After breakfast of rice porridge and sliced apple, we decide to head to Baisha, a Hmong village a few kilometers off. As usual, it's hectic getting a ride out of town; nobody's interested. Finally, our hotel manager, who wants to join us, helps hire a car. From the moment we set foot in Baisha, we feel relaxed. It's the slow pace, the nurture of Nature, the immediate sense of time warp. Perched in descending slopes, the village falls away into evaporating mists. Smoke drifts from eaves, blue peaks fade into haze. A woodpecker knocks; a mallet echoes it. We come to a group of carpenters working on a new house, all by hand: pegged joinery, adzed and planed fir planks, peeled honey-colored posts and beams. Some of the men are dressed in indigo, white browbands, shaven heads, hair in topknots. Others wear sport shirts, polyester trousers, Han style. They are obviously proud of their work as they cheerfully measure, notch, and plane rough-sawn boards. They smile as we inspect the redolent, freshly hewn structure. Liao Jing notes our interest and mentions a famous carpenter, Lu Ban, a historical figure, contemporary with Confucius, who was raised to a deity, patron of carpenters. In doorways women spin thread, sort indigo leaves, starch skirts, fold long bolts of pounded cloth. Outside is a row of skeletal maize-drying racks, bare, save for a couple of crows. The corn has been taken in to be shucked. Below, in all directions:

> weightless ridges
> my pen too heavy.

We stop in a shed where thick rounds of harvested bamboo are being sawed into uniform lengths, split with machetes, pleated into boxes used to ship local citrus. Up a trail stand three or four pole and plank corn cribs. They overlook the slope like sentinels, like the wooden drum towers of Bali. Suddenly a boy runs out from a group of houses and waves us over to a man who wants to show us, for a yuan, his muzzle-loading rifle. The man hands it over, we begin to examine it, he gets anxious, grabs it back. It's loaded! Now that he's got it, he gives a wide smile, points it to the sky, and WHAMMM, fires it with a tremendous roar of white smoke that envelopes us all. Then silence, the jangle of a pony, wind bell dangling from an eave:

> around
> the bell, blue sky
> ringing.

Leaving Baisha, we stop in a villager's home for a shot of rice wine. It's dark, smoky; we hunker around hot coals into which our host places cassava to roast while he fetches the spirits. He returns with the drink, and pours. Liao Jing remarks: "He respects you." Why? I ask. "Your glass is full. If your glass is only half full you are not so honored." One cup and another is refilled, we drink up, eat our cassava—a nice belly warmer, along with the 30-proof wine, in the slight chill. We buy a liter for two yuan, thank our host, walk into the light. Amber dragonflies dart at water funneling from bamboo irrigation pipes. Step by step it flashes down the mountain . . .

> drink stops time,
> brings the land
> into light.

Han Shan, T'ao Ch'ien. I get a sense of their mountains, their minds, how a morning could last a thousand years. Rustic joys, cloudy wine cup, a hint of truth above the dust and noise. Nanao Sakaki once suggested: "If you want to feel Japanese spirit, walk into rice fields after drinking sake." On the way to Yagul, Peter Garland smiled over a shot of mescal: "You'll see the ruins better this way." In Bali a glass of brem heightens the trance dances; a little arak brings the duendes from their ravines. In Cuba, rum gets the body rippling with the lavish canefields, the luscious roll of a Camaygueña's hips. In Nong Khai, drink Mekong whiskey; in Luang Prabang, Lao khao; in Muktinath, chang. Along the Maine coast, hearty ale; on Ruby Beach, Zinfandel; at Nepenthe, Chardonnay. Jim Harrison notes that "good wine increases the best aspects of camaraderie and sweetens the tongue for conversation." Wang Wei, whose nature it was to be "clean and quiet," watched wild landscapes emerge from his brush, capping the night with apricot wine.

Walking out of Baisha, white clouds, blue ravines:

> a gap in the hills
> heatwaves rising
> where locusts cry.

Back in Congjiang, Renée notes: "Today in a stranger's house we ate, drank, warmed ourselves. Our host demanded nothing, said nothing, simply crouched with us, full of good cheer, taking it all in. We liked each other." I am glad for this, the solidarity that travel engenders. I see myself, 10 years old—Kodak camera, spiral notebook—hiking granite domes in the Sierra Nevada. Fifteen years old, bumming rides, listening to stories of hay farmers, going back to those same domes. Twenty-two years old, hitching through southern Chile: deep forests, broken islands, misting rain; the archipelago where I first hiked a volcano, tasted apple wine, made love, knew solidarity with complete strangers in humble plankboard houses. A sense of recklessness, vulnerability. To get down, come together, be alone, record particulars, organize the picture, let the emotional portrait emerge; the sweetness, the darkness become ink—and shine.

A round of dark Hubein beer, and another. Liao Jing comments on the accent here: "So different, the locals have trouble understanding me." When she orders dinner, instead of bamboo shoots and baby potatoes, we get pole beans with tiny cap mushrooms. But so what? They're absolutely tender, delicious—as is the bok choy with sliced garlic bathed in a sweet chile sauce. The main plate is a whole lake fish, crispy fried in spicy red sauce. After dinner we cross the river to the more traditional side of town. Bars, bakeries, pharmacies, shoe repair shops, a dusty bookstore, an ancient barbershop painted eerie green, dim fly-spotted light bulb over big red chair, something like a pump handle attached to it. Under the mirror are razors, straps, flasks of cyanide-blue and blood-red antiseptics. On the dentist's desk, a pair of teeth in a glass. Back over the river to our hotel on the new side of town, a giant billboard shows Congjiang's future: a lucrative tourist resort with a sparkling white octopus of high-rise hotels surrounding a fairground where "Miao and Dong Minority People will Celebrate for You."

> on the river's breeze
> cricket chorus
> between karaoke bars.


## 22 NOVEMBER: ZHAOXING

The oldest Dong village in Guizhou and the largest in China is 80 kilometers from Congjiang in a magnificent valley tucked into deeply forested hills rising 1,000 meters. To the north, terraced rice paddies finger through a narrow canyon; out of it runs a river spanned by several wind-and-rain bridges. Five pagoda drum towers, rebuilt after the Cultural Revolution, rise over wood houses and cobble walks whose stone is worked into intricate fish and flower designs. We settle into a pegged wooden guest house, then wander out to walk the bridges, admire an old, painted opera stage, watch women pound and dye cloth. Some wave us into their houses to examine textiles. On market street are bins of lichens, dried fruit, hand-forged farm tools, a can of gunpowder, a wheelbarrow, a display of dusty western toilets.

In Zhaoxing we shake off the dirt of the world, regain our senses. People are welcoming, the land cared for. Renée relaxes over a hearty soup: "For me too much of China lacks sensuousness. My pores don't open as they do in Bali or Cuba. Instead I want to close down, protect myself." Zhaoxing is the perfect antidote for closed pores. Its isolation and quiet pace reminds us of the last episode in Kurasawa's *Dreams*. A village of waterwheels and handmade houses, orchards and flowered shrines; a hands-to-earth realm where people dwell harmoniously with nature and each other. At the story's end, an old man comments on how modern people prioritize convenience, invent things that make them unhappy, and live in pollution. Clean air and water rank high on his list, right up there with the joy of being satisfied after a long day of meaningful work.

But this is the very world held in contempt by so much of China's hierarchy. "Quaint, backwards, slow to progress, unable to change. Minority people, difficult people." In *Behind the Wall*, Colin Thubron writes about a train depot in Xining where a huge canvas of Mao greets China's minority races. "Vanquished Tibetans, despised Miao, oppressed Hui were smiling round him in grateful reverence. At any moment it seemed, he would raise his hand in papal blessing as his superior wisdom and moral purity led them, all clean in their folk-dress, to the brightness of the Revolution."

Before our China trip, a student from Shanghai in one of our poetry classes constantly corrected me on Li Po, insisting: "Li Bai, Li Bai, that is his proper name!" When Renée announced we were going to China, she asked where. "Xishuangbanna, Yunnan, Guizhou." There was a look of shock. "Oh that's not China, not Han people. Very dangerous, they can kill you." I smiled. What if we were two Chinese headed to the U.S. and told someone from Delaware we were going to Hopi and they replied. "Oh that's not America, not American people. They can kill you."

A back street of evenly laid stone, carefully chiseled and fitted. A group of girls jump rope in a complex ballet of side skips, hops, and spins. They challenge us, we back away laughing. Two boys with runny noses and seatless trousers look on. Two old guys with wrinkled leather faces under dark Mao caps stagger up. A bit tipsy, they're feeling brave. One offers to sell a bamboo-stem pipe, lauding its worth. A bent witch of a grandma clumps up in scruffy tennis shoes. She holds out a sweat-polished wood tobacco case, indicating that I can hang it from the pipe, assuming I'll purchase it. But why do I want it? Because some other tourist did, and she believes I'm a replica of that tourist? I hand it all back and do a jig which sets children and viejos laughing—but not the witch. Shortly, the old guys figure I'm a little too wacked for their morning, and off they bumble, with a Chaplin hobble, toward another wine shop.

The only other non-Chinese tourists in Zhaoxing are two female couples. The first, a laid-back pair, Japanese and Korean, are sharing a beer on the steps of an eatery. Liao Jing discovers they speak Mandarin, are studying in Kunming, and are here to sightsee and practice Mandarin with people who speak it as a second language. A nice radiance from this couple. In a smattering of English, that tell us they're going to Diping to see the famous Qing-dynasty wind-and-rain bridge. The other couple, two Spanish women, has precisely the opposite energy. They look around constantly as they speak, jab at their food, gobble it nervously. Their hands hardly leave their bulging fanny packs unguarded as they proceed to bore us with a list of places visited or about to be visited. Their only questions: "Anything worth it up the road? How much time can we do it in?"

I'm left to wonder just exactly *how* these women had been where they were, or why, with such rush, they were doing it at all. One seemed to have been assigned the task of "picture taking," eyeballing everything relentlessly through a digital camera; the other did the planning, toying with a miniature cell phone, always one step ahead of herself. After we part, I buy a stick of cane and find a place to sit:

> mountain warmth
> my back pressed
> to a stone wall.

## 22 NOVEMBER: ZHAOXING

Last night I got a sudden flu-like chill after dinner, crawled into my sleeping bag under two quilts with all my clothes on, downed mint tea, took yin chiao, and stayed quiet despite the raucous smoking and drinking downstairs: a party of drunken Chinese "officials" babbling all-at-once loud talk. We soon learned that these provincial honchos were in Zhaoxing to discuss ways to promote tourism. They had hired a Dong dance troupe to perform. After dark the inn emptied; dancers and musicians assembled in the plaza. I napped, regained strength, and off we wandered to the performance.

The traditional dress, singing, circular dance movements, and pipe playing of the Dong performers were excellent, but sadly all was constantly interrupted by the impolite state officials who, in suits and ties, loaded to the gills, demanded that we foreigners sit with them on a front row bench. Embarrassed, I begrudgingly took a seat between these clapping drunks who flashed their cameras and intermittently stood up, staggering into the circle to whoop and gyrate around the dancers. (Imagine doing this at a Hopi kachina dance!) At one point one of the provincial honchos looked at us and yelled, "Welcome to *our* China!" as he made patting motions over the head of a female performer. I left the bench immediately to stand in the shadows with a troupe of musicians waiting to perform. It was way over the top for me, these officials who had succeeded in buying "their" minorities to entertain them for the night, eager to flaunt their pride in front of the gringos. It was especially hard to bear after 30 years of attending Hopi and Zuni ceremonials, where utmost respect is required, no cameras allowed, the word "minority" not tolerated, and the people belong to sovereign nations, their tribal names intact. Adding to my disgust, these same officials returned to our inn to resume their drinking, at which point Renée and I packed up and bolted, much to Liao Jing's concern. A simpler inn down the road provided a quiet night's sleep. The wooden structure was solidly built, warmer than the first, and the family quite pleasant.

Today we walk, relax, make plans to catch a morning bus to Guangxi Province: Yangshuo, and the Li River, a place I've always wanted to see. Strolling a narrow path, a woman's song lifts from the paddies. She's harvesting greens into a basket:

> the daikon picker
> without looking up
> knows we're passing.

Zhaoxing, with its idyllic setting and balanced lifestyle, gives hope in our disorderly world; but it also heightens the inevitable mourning a traveler experiences as witness to a planet under siege. Such a small, tucked away circle among the big "civilization" with its need to progress, expand, industrialize, militarize—no matter the toll on physical lives, nature, the imagination, the right to move freely across the planet. IF YOU ARE NOT ALARMED YOU ARE NOT PAYING ATTENTION reads a bumper sticker back home. The need for vigilance is paramount.

Another film comes to mind. Tarkovsky's *Sacrifice*, in which a writer finds himself alienated in a world where humans have left the plow for the sword. He is surrounded by a society dependent not on each other or nature, but on fear, aggression, brutality, and lethal weapons for keeping power. War has gone beyond being part of daily life; it is culminating in the annihilation of the planet. The film brings to mind a world created not only by the terrorist attacks of Islamic fundamentalists, but by Bush's attack on Iraq's secular regime—no evidence linking our former buddy, Saddam Hussein, with our present foe, bin Laden, or with weapons of mass destruction. Clearly, the obsession to overthrow Hussein, and fixing the facts to do so (the weapons of mass destruction hoax) was planned long ago.

By picking on a country that did not attack us, and giving the death sentence—bombs, occupation, terror, torture—to hundreds of thousands of Iraqis, the majority of them civilians, America has arrogantly ushered in chaos, revenge, and an alarming disharmony among people. To be an American abroad having to explain this ignorance isn't fun; nor is having to return to a country run by an ego-inflated, Catch-22, can't-back-down junta of faith-based militants who tickle the mushroom cloud, put clamps on the media, encourage corporate takeover, confine wealth to the elite, and wrap the rest with surveillance, poverty, and heads-in-the-sand "education."

So much talk of good and evil. But a righteous idea of "good" consisting of iron-fisted doctrine certainly smells of "evil." Things are going quickly bankrupt; mother nature's on the run. The "well-behaved" men and profit-monger Evangelists have put the death warrants out, called for assassinations, and imprisoned themselves and their followers with fixed norms, using schoolmaster whips for those who challenge their authority. Analogies abound: Imperial Rome, Babylon, China in the fourth and 10th centuries.

In Zhaoxing I am reminded that peace is enough. Those old Chinese poets who took to the hills after suffering the hells of collapsing dynasties, murder, massacre, misrule, heavy taxation, and debauchery, knew that a person of courage would never encourage violence. What better display of courage than to *refuse* violence?! Li Po—himself arrested, imprisoned, and banished, fed up with his own era—wrote a poem about a previous one, about never-ending war:

FIGHTING SOUTH OF THE WALL

Last year we fought where the San-kan flows,
this year it's Ts'ung River. We've washed our swords
in the T'iao-chih sea, grazed our horses
on T'ien Shan's snows.

Thousands of miles our campaign goes,
our armies worn and old. But the Mongols view killing
as they do plowing their land, sowing our bones
in fields of yellow sand.

A Qin Dynasty emperor built the Great Wall
to seal them out. Now, its the Han Dynasty
but we still light signal fires, keep beacons ablaze
that can never go out.

No end to forced campaigns and war.
Hand to hand, men fight til death,
horses stumble, cry out to heaven. Crows and kites
tear at our remains, carry them to dead trees.

Soldiers' blood smears tangled grasses
while the generals, without plan, keep at it.
Clearly, war is an ill-omened tool. Great sages
never waited for the need to arise.

To say certain moments in Zhaoxing have been idyllic doesn't mean
I've confused people's hard lives with bliss, nor mistaken raw poverty
for perfection. But I've seen an intelligent and caring bond created by
the sharing of common tasks: growing and harvesting food; maintaining
woods, springs, tillable swales; directing the course of water in a
communal way. Down below the world overpopulates, tangles its gears
with haste, rage, fraud, hatred, unjustified war, waste, stolen proportions
of wealth in the hands of a few. The arrogance and ideologies of the
Cultural Revolution did not spare these farmers, yet in the end—as
their resistance grew—it could neither incorporate nor obliterate them.
Their language and songs remain strong. The hills sparkle, stones are
quarried and set, wild geese land in the river, clouds roll from the canyon,
peach trees swell.

The work of the hands remains the stuff of prayer, meditation,
gratitude for life. The farmer's anxieties are certainly not those of rushed
people whose lives are made vulnerable and complicated under artificial
systems. To be "pressed" for time is one thing; to be engaged in the

cycle of seasons, with space to do all, or to do nothing if one so desires, is another. Yes, certain moments *have* been idyllic: a child with the face of semi-precious stone learning to reel in a kite, a kingfisher skimming clear-water rapids, a waterwheel creaking its spill into hand-worked fields, the ghost of Wang Wei brushing ink onto mulberry paper high above the road's end. I could take to the mountains, let my hair go white, write a simple poem while others try to explain the impossible. But isn't that exactly the life I've chosen back home?

## NIGHT OF NOVEMBER 22: ZHAOXING

Not to be a travel writer, but a writer who travels. One who leaves the nest, takes a double-eyed look, comes back with another head. The journal is an eye inside the heart, an ear tuned to the outer world and to the one inside. Work through words, find stance in the journey. Turn down the lamp, crickets wake. Clear out the weeds, a water lily blooms. Coal dust on the lens, walk into the wind. Monsoon deluge, nap in a mountain shrine. Halfway around the world, finish a poem, fill the pen. No applause, just the teapot lifting its lid:

> while others go about
> their computer screens
> I find my way in the dark.

I think of Pablo Neruda tonight, a poet at home on earth in contrast to so many poets at home only in the academy. He walked new continents with the same fervor as he did his own native streets. His journey, with its questions and confrontations, was a means of discovering a new self as well as opening up dialogue with fellow world citizens. I like his exuberance, curiosity, love of the earth, the body. I read him, as I do Li Po or Li Ch'ing-chao—as an antidote to the squareness, the dourness of our times . . .

Let us draw our tired bones together.
In the half-sun of long days
Let us forget the unfaithful ones,
the unfeeling friends.

The sun wavers among the pines.
Let us forget those who are unaware.
There are lands within the land,
small uncared-for countries.

Let us not think of the satisfied ones,
let us forget their false teeth.
Let the sensitive ones sleep
on their fine feather beds.

One must know particular stones
full of fractures and secrets.
Let us forget with generosity
those who cannot love us.

It's good to have a change of clothes,
of skin, of hair, of work,

to be part of clean air,
to disdain all oligarchies.

Let us have a talk with roots
and disenchanted waves.
Let us forget about hurry,
the teeth of the efficient.

Let us forget about the shadowy
miscellany of those who wish us ill.
Let us make a profession of being earth bound
let us touch the earth with our entire soul.

(Excerpts from "Sonata With Some Pines" from *Extravagaria*)


## 23 NOVEMBER: YANGSHUO

The promised six-hour ride into Guangxi Province (to Guilin, to hop a mini bus another hour south to Yangshuo) was well over eight, easily ranking among the worst travel of my life—i.e., crossing the ragged Andean cordilleras, Lima to Cusco by truck, piled in with Quechua farmers for two days of perilous death-defying switchbacks; ditto a two-day crammed-to-the-gills Himalayan ride skirting rebel activity along Kashmir-Pakistan cease-fire line, over Zoji La, through dizzy crags and vomit-inducing cliffs, to Ladakh.

Our bus today didn't cover as perilous terrain, but the edgy bald-tire wheel-slipping under-construction one-lane gravel-road ride (who defers to whom around which blind corner is largely a matter of fate) was a five-star horror in other ways. The arrogant hammerhead of a driver, barely into his twenties, paid more attention to his concubine-of-a-thrill, straddling the engine cowling next to him, than to the road. A devilish prankster, he'd often display his machismo by slowing to a crawl for a potential passenger along the road, turning the wheels deliberately close to a cliff edge; or, on the middle of a bridge, edging the bus toward the railing, braking just at the last moment for a hens-in-a-basket hitchhiker, looking back to see our reaction, smiling fiendishly. The driver's girlfriend would surely have driven Liao Jing mad. Until now we'd yet to meet an unreserved Chinese woman, but here she was, a painted ornament haloed in fumes leaking through the engine cowling, around which she wrapped her long legs, occasionally raising her tight-jeaned ass into the air for the pleasure of the entire bus as she deliberately dropped and reached for her Chinese tootsie rolls, which she chewed for awhile then spit toward a half-cracked window, usually with a miss. Back in her movie-star posture—legs crossed, breasts arched outward—she'd fire up yet another ciggie, tilt her head, sweep back her hair, and blow smoke toward the dangerous metal ceiling bar to which the (promised) video screen was once bolted.

And the passengers? Each was a knobby backwater bumpkin right out of a fairy tale: dirty, coarsely shouting non-stop over the unmuffled engine, chain smoking (windows rolled up), heaving butts, sunflower shells, and wads of spit to the floor, dust slowly powdering their dark, threadbare attire. In 40 years of travels I can't recall another journey (save for a Greyhound in West Virginia's coal country) where I felt more unacknowledged, purposely ignored. Eerie, indeed, to realize how truly vague and dangerous it is to be among humans (wild animals are more predictable and lovelier to watch). If either of us were suddenly taken sick, I felt the door would have opened and we both would have been given a solid push. Eight hours of bad curves, bald tires, shouting voices, and lung smoke; then, just as we sputter down the long cliff-hanging grade into Guilin, the driver decides to stop, gas up, have the bus washed (the aisles of trash remain untouched): another 45 minutes, and only 15 minutes from our final destination:

> NO SMOKING
> the driver
> lights up first.

Yangshuo's lodging is superb, the place well-accustomed to visitors. We lodge at the Lianlian (Y80), an exceptionally clean hotel, up from the Li River on Xi Jie. The accommodating young manager answers politely as we comment on the absence of foreigners in Yangshuo. "It's the SARS scare." Deflated after our bus ride, we bathe, recoup with tea and herbal concoctions to counter the ungodly amount of cigarette smoke we've swallowed. Secretly, I entertain another lifetime of simply staying home, tending the garden, setting stone, entertaining the grandkids, and being a prep-chef for Renée's superb cooking. Given another life doing that, I'd eagerly spend the rest of this one on the road. Realistically, though, there is only one lifetime. In it I seek to balance homemaker and wanderer, an ideal that requires no full-time job, literary award, fellowship, or graduate degree.

In his memoir, *Off to the Side*, Jim Harrison says to take to the road is to experience a dislocation in which we deliberately isolate ourselves to discover answers that evade us, or remain too obvious in familiar surroundings. "Perhaps the dominant advantage of travel for a writer is to pull oneself out of the nest in whose comfort the vision can become self-serving, truncated, the nest itself losing oxygen with time so that the life lived becomes drowsy. It's comic to look back and see how much you've missed by immediately making a habit out of your location." As a painter, I thrive on particular landscapes, geology, geography. Not just the view from our home in New Mexico over slanted high-desert mesas to the Jemez caldera with its sexy volcanic humps, but the view into mythic karst formations of Halong Bay, Phra Nang, Pinar del Rio, and Yangshuo: places that certainly reconfirm, in reality, what the imagination has, since childhood, already revealed.

A sign on the stone wall next to the hotel door:

FREE FACE MESSAGE
MEDICINAL HEAD WASH
ROMANCE ATMOSPHERE

## 24 NOVEMBER: YANGSHUO

First real coffee since leaving Kunming. It comes with a huge bowl of sweet pears and apples, cheese omelette, home-made bread, tangerine juice. Over breakfast, a Chinese couple from Guangzhou chuckles at our travel descriptions: "Oh, Chinese from Guizhou very uneducated. Full of bad habits, small view. No idea of how anyone else lives."

It's as if we've just described a trip, as two Chinese tourists would to Americans, of the Arkansas backcountry. Talking with this couple, I still can't tell if China's growth, its fanatical obsession for "futurizing" (leveled mountains, militarized border zones, flooded towns, industrial purgatories, choked cities, defunct monasteries, over-hyped tourist attractions) is really an over-compensation for its history of dynastic collapses. Has China historically been obsessed with "the next" or had its emphasis (until Mao) been on preserving worthy aspects of each dynasty, carrying them slowly into the future? Pearly mists effervesce from phantom crags behind town:

> a raindrop—
> inside it another
> has fallen.

While we enjoy Yangshuo, Steve and Jacquie are now heading back to Guiyang with Liao Jing. I wonder what she thought of the crazy gringos whom she was obliged to guide with diligence and respect? Though she did exceptionally well, it feels much better to be on our own, enjoying sidetracks, fumbling rather than following a straight line. There are language roadblocks, sure. But for two poets it's a joy to have to piece together the difficulties of tones and glyphs, to learn the character for "eggplant" by copying it off a menu board, then learn to pronounce it so we can eat in the untouristed part of town. In Yangshuo a pharmacist, as eager to learn English as I am Mandarin, corrects me on some phrases and translates a few characters from her herbal dictionary as I linger after a purchase of medicinal tea.

Today we travel to Fuli, where we catch a mini bus to Xingping, further up the Li, where we'll hire a boat for an afternoon river trip. Both of us are feeling happy, light of spirit. Last night, bright moon between shallow clouds. In a narrow alley, someone rinsing silk in a wood tub. Near the pebbly shallows of the Li, a white egret under a spreading tree. Encapsulated in the moment I wanted only a bowl of rice, a silent cottage at the mouth of a gorge, woven catkins for a gate, morning glories trailing up my woodpile. Again, I caught myself thinking of home. We don't have these abruptly rising limestone formations, but we do have the sweep of mesas, a drifting volcanic island on the horizon, morning glories around the cedar stack, crickets in the eaves, gourds climbing the shed—and the privilege, in our isolation, of when and how we want to mingle in society.

## 24 NOVEMBER: LI RIVER

At a bend on a trail along the Li Jiang, the woman guiding us to the boat launch stops, turns, takes a 20-yuan bill from her pocket (I think she's about to demand an extra tip) and holds it over the flowing water. Behind are the exact mountains pictured on the bill, the famous Li Jiang karst forms jutting hundreds of feet over the shore. We hike down the banks to pay the boatman and are motored out onto the river. Clean air in lungs, eyes washed with sunlit breeze, diminished in stature, we regain our true place in the world. No war, no chaos. Only mirror upon mirror of vine-wrapped limestone towers, leaning pagodas, shapely goddesses, humpback ogres. One unkempt peak reaches as if longing for a lover. Another, almost a twin, bends a wild head of hair toward it. As a child I squiggled these same shapes with a thick-lead pencil to graph inner rhythms I couldn't put into words. Now I've slipped behind the screen of time to enter the scenes I drew. Meanwhile, Renée, who's been plagued by a sore throat, is suddenly at peace, crosslegged on the prow. "Everything is all right exactly as is," she later recalls. "That was my enlightenment on the Li."

Our boatman takes the wheel through depths and narrows, rapids and pools. The ever-dynamic peaks vibrate with prismed auras. In mottled haze, their lofty forms repeat over and over as they recede across an unwinding scroll into a backdrop of lavender wash. Shapes retreat, edge forward, sometimes move both ways at once. Often their outlines spread into abstract fantasy as if watercolored on silk. Just when the composition begins to become predictable, a sudden interval of blank sky gives pause. The eye is released from subject. Imagination is left to invent.

As the boat ripples along, each tower of thickening, thinning brush strokes changes face as the angle shifts. What seemed a rider on a stallion is now a dragon tossing at sea. Through the centuries, the Chinese have named them all: Fishtail Summit, Lion Watching Nine Horses, Tortoise Climbing Hill, Eight Supernaturals on Raft, Woman Behind Screen, Nine Oxen Ridge, Happy Marriage Pavilion. As we drift and I madly sketch, I name a few of my own: Crazy Face, Crocodile Jaw, Bickering Couple, Sitting Frog, Cock Rock, Fasting Sage, Lonely Lady, Dripping Mound.

The day is mild, halcyon. The mountains just keep coming, rising, falling, and with them it's simply astounding to be alive; unbelievable, actually, that anyone could be alive, our world such a mess. Sprays of bamboo catch the breeze, fan into gold. The boat passes into deep purple; skin chills; the air tastes of reeds. Then the sun floods in again, ricochets from river, turns an entire cliff into a mirror of ripples brushed by a master calligrapher. On the shore is a grove of grapefruit trees, in its shadows a lashed-together raft. A man naps between nets and lines:

> amid floating lotus
> a hooked fish
> slapping.

I think of Wang Wei, his later years, tranquillity a priority, the mind left to unravel in the breeze. I think of our amigo Bari, gone to Mongolia. Artist, naturalist, investigative wanderer. How far will the winds take him, and will they bring him back with a Mongolian wife? I think of Jacquie on the Mekong, recording details of passing scenery. Or Ponheary in Angkor, that certain expression on her face (on so many Cambodian faces), like it could never fully recover from what it had seen. I watch Renée greet the stairs of a teakwood inn with bare feet, greet the owner with folded palms. I see Ed and Jo Ann packing for Afghanistan. Ira running out of breath in Amsterdam. Peter on the bandstand in Tlacotalpan. Head in a dream, my eyes return to the river:

> is it the water
> or the stones at the bottom
> moving?

Back in Xingping, orange peels dry on racks in the shade. Rats, a local delicacy, are for sale in wire cages. Above a shoe shop, a girl preens herself in a window over a sign: "Slippers Made Here of Local Wood that Prevents Athlete's Foot & Bike Tyres. We Move Nails to Adjust Your Foot Size." Songbirds in hanging baskets. Saddlebags, abacus, broom against adobe wall. Little girls roll hoops. Purple thistles burst from the cobble. Bucket of quail eggs, cellophane kite, set of drills. Boat paddle, cowbell, hand-forged door hinges. Walking sticks, rice bowls, coils of wire. Dustpan, wheel hub, bicycle chain. All set out on white canvas along a dusty street:

> daikon seeds
> in a vendor's hand
> —autumn mountains.

Bus back to Yangshuo. A gift from the boatman pasted in my journal: red cigarette wrapper with miniature, gold-framed painting of Li River and karst peaks. A man practices his English: "Americans? Oh America, that's where George Bush goes boom!" Korean traveler says he got tired of the States, now headed back to his home village on the southern sea. "Started out in Pakistan. Hindu Kush to Qinghai Plateau. Silk Route to Xishuangbanna. Jinghong to Guilin. All friendly people." A Chinese couple from New York City also rides the bus. "Lived on Mulberry Street until Trade Tower attack; we now like it in Hong Kong." In my journal I copy out the character "shan": mountain. Beside it I place the character "shui": water. Shan shui: mountains and rivers, "landscape."

"Landscape" in English implies something static, to be looked at, confined to geologic increments, qualified with adjectives ("stunning," etc). In Chinese "landscape" reconfirms that I am an integral part. I float within its all-enveloping Consciousness. We pulsate together, one-same Organism. To define the world with adjectives is futile, but I can come near to her with poetry, walk in with my body, swim with her rhythms, let her dynamism enfold me, become her Breath Force (Qi), fly with cosmic energies. When she writhes, retreats, exhales, warms herself in the sun, her curves and swales—like the temple of my woman—become the gardens of the Forbidden City, the plums of the Summer Palace, the Axis of the Mundo. Mountains and rivers: Eternal ever-recombining regenerative SOURCE.

## 25 NOVEMBER: YANGSHUO

Renée's throat is much better. Rented bicycles today, headed for Yulong He River Valley, two kilometers toward Moon Hill then onto a dirt track 10 kilometers between looming hills, meandering harvested rice fields along the river. Tombs in tangerine groves, haystacks nodding in mustard fields, red-papered Chinese script on wood doors. Yellow houses, yellow faces, yellow earth under purple cane, yellow handlebars on our Crocodile-brand bikes. I'd be buried in yellow, live a life of lacquered red, die turquoise (after bursts of chartreuse, periods of indigo, flare of lemon in high-altitude blue). Memory is alabaster, future is ebony. Sex a bolt of sapphire resting in ruby.

Cold water gurgles through willows where one village meets another. Dry umber land. Thick, winey plum orchards. Memories of

Oaxacan sierra: bare-breasted girl drying herself with pink towel in full view, upstairs farmhouse window. Memories of Cuba: white donkey scuffing a hoof in front of a corner bar in Trinidad. Bartender offers a stale, rum-dipped baguette in his outstretched hand. Donkey scuffs a heel to thank him. We park bikes, rest against a haystack. Brittle smells engulf our flesh:

> parched fields
> yellow so bright
> it's blue.

## NOVEMBER'S END: YANGSHUO

A sure way to find out if you love or hate someone is to take to the road together. I'm lucky to be blessed with a kindred spirit who's willing to abandon the practical for the raw. I think of us in so many places, immutably together, yet exactly unlike each other: on the jagged crest of Gokyo-ri; in the subway to Harlem; at the Dos Hermanos Bar with Lorca; along the Big Sur with Jeffers; in Tenganan for Indra's feast; at Shungopavi for the coming of the kachinas; under the spray of Tana Barak reciting our vows; leaving Te Tieu, upriver to the Perfume Pagoda; in Kbal Spean hiking the thousand-linga stream; in the Ho rain forest looking for bear; in the Weminuche wilderness climbing the ragged edge of Uncompaghre; in Pangboche watching snow banners stream from Ama Dablam; in Puri Lumbung glimpsing the Java Sea through clove hills; on the banks of Ma Ganga watching women scatter flowers to the rising sun.

Wandering. An act of renunciation and of solidarity. Traveling. A practice and a process, neither for escape nor entertainment, in which one seeks source and renewal in the inevitable mysteries of place and people. Pilgrimage. A symbolic hoedown. A way of life, a way of poetry, a conspiracy. The art of breaking social barriers, sabotaging the headlines with truth. Wherever we are, this is our fuel.

Decades ago, Moritz Thomsen turned me on to Claude Levi-Strauss. Which book, I don't remember. But a phrase stayed with me which I've written many times over, especially before traveling: "If you wish to wrest something from destiny you must venture into that perilous margin-country where the norms of society count for nothing and the demands and guarantees of the group are no longer valid."

Once, under Delicate Arch, I lost grip on a sheer sandstone cliff and slid ever so slowly to peril, frozen in mind and body, until I realized I could remake the presence of fear into a great leap of energy, whereby I shot upward, and fingerhold by fingerhold, retrieved level land. In the margin-country sometimes your own partner cannot be of aid.

> late moon
> each thought the other
> had the key.

Coffee at Yang Di's. Goateed man wheels pink squash through blue shade; dragonfly inspects red pajamas on clothesline; sliced persimmons dry over bins of fungus, snails, chestnuts, cabbage heads, skinned rabbits, silk slippers. A boy chisels headstones for the dead. A shopkeeper lights an eight-foot string of firecrackers leading into his doorway. We finish breakfast, return to Lianlian. Shower, pack, say goodbye to proprietor and mother:

> the old lady
> at the desk—
> exactly my age.

Two-hour taxi ride to airport, via traffic-clogged Guilin: Cigarette Trade Hotel, Up-date Inn, Fish Head Chaffy, See View Crunch House, Warrior Hug-all, Soft Glade Eye Soap, Tourish Glutton, Red Capitalism Cafe, Slef Challeng Romance, Phone Jade Lady @ Odds and Wonders. We reach the airport in plenty of time. Check-in is swift and easy, despite the razor blade I keep with my art supplies. The security team catches it immediately on their screen (U.S. officials didn't). At first I don't understand them as they rustle through my pack, saying: "Sorry. You have cut face? Cut face?" Then it hits me. They mean: "razor for shaving." I unwrap my brushes and inks; they apologize for having to confiscate the blade. "Next time check under" (meaning, put it with non-carry-on items).

We head to gate #9 (*number nine… number nine… number nine…*) for the Guilin-Kunming-Bangkok flight. A shop in the lounge sells local products: taro cakes, chestnut crackers, candied longan, laurel-flower wine. A bookstore offers herbal dictionaries, poetry, silk-cased novels, a Li River sketchbook, bonsai manuals, a well-thumbed-through photography book titled *Art Poses*. Chinese models straddling the line between art and porn: nubile girls; legs askew, heads thrown back, eyes seductively fixed on viewer.

The real surprise is the calligrapher next door. Renée discovers him under a sign: "Write Your Name Chinese $4." A light goes off inside me. I waste no time approaching his table to ask if he could write, instead of my name, a poem. He doesn't understand at first, but when he hears Tu Fu, Wang Wei, Li Po, he smiles and calls over the bookstore lady who speaks some English and clarifies my wish. He nods, fumbles through a drawer, fishes out a bilingual xerox of a Li Po poem. Perfect! He sets to work with brush and ink and in minutes has the poem—he knows it by memory—brushed out on a scroll, stamped with his chops:

> Climb Guan Qui pavilion
> The yellow sun is setting behind the mountain
> The yellow river flows into the ocean.
>
> If one wants to gain a grand view
> For thousands of miles afar, he must climb
> To another level of the tower.

Elated beyond words, I bow, thank him profusely, and pay the agreed-upon $7. He is obviously pleased that I wanted a poem rather than my name. Renée is beaming: "Can you believe it? The scroll you were looking for all over China, with a poem you didn't expect, in an airport at Gate #9, while waiting to board a flight!"

The poem is exactly right. It not only runs parallel to Renée's Rongjiang dream (remove the soot to see the beauty), it provides another dimension (to see above your own nose, try another level) to Bashō's:

"Keep your mind high in the world of true understanding, but don't forget the value of what's down low."

Above the clouds, to Bangkok via Kunming. As soymilk jujube drinks are passed out by a trance-like pair of attendants, we peruse Air Yunnan's *Shangri La* magazine:

> ENJOY NEW EXPERIENCE EATING CULTURE.
> WHAT YOU REALLY NEED IS NOT DELICIOUS FOOD
> BUT BEST RECOLLECTION.
>
> LAY YOUR IMAGINATION ON THE CLOUDS.
> IF YOU ARE DREAMER GO TO LIJIANG. IF HEDON, DALI.
> IF ADVENTURER YOU CAN RELEASE CREATIVITY
> IN THE JUNGLE OF XISHUANGBANNA.
>
> EACH CAN BE MORE WONDERFUL THAN HER DESIRE
> IN THE OMNI PRESENT CULTURAL ATMOSPHERE.
> IT BRINGS MUCH MORE INTELLIGENCE TO WHO LOVES IT.
>
> GOOD HOLIDAYS IS SPENT WITH PEOPLE
> WHOSE NOTIONS OF TIME IS VAGUER THAN YOURS.
>
> FROM SUCH KIND OF CULTURE
> NOBODY WANT TO ESCAPE.

PRACHUAP KHIRI KHAN,
THAILAND: through white haze
nameless Mountains
washed with surf

Love in the afternoon. The old
chinese hotel Rocks on its posts. We become
TENDER ANIMALS while shadows grow deep
DOWN in the garden children Bat plastic
BALLS against the WALL. Espresso machine
fizzes TriUMPHantly: Twenty to 5.

# THAILAND

*Poetry is the measure,*
*as it is the life*
CID CORMAN

*when the story*
*gets going. Hang on*
JOANNE KYGER

I look into the stars, 36,000 feet, jet stream pushing against me. Blackness. Tokyo 2000 miles away. Aleutians ice jagged under my tongue. Yellow wart on my finger, blue auras around passenger heads silhouetted by transoceanic movie. English becomes Japanese. Tomorrow becomes today. My white shirt is silent, each cuff asleep. Hands keep company with their own fingers, body crosses the line. Old self burns out. I'm a cracked pot, shooting star disentangled from its tale. Not of that body, those associations, but of this thought, these sensations. Wind stands still, flesh configures anew. What city did we leave from, what consciousness left behind? Lift the shade, follow star threads, night's cryptogram, inkjet reminiscences. The weight of a pencil is the same as the weight of the plane. I remember mother teaching me to read, a Wyeth illustration on the facing page. Tiny pinpoints of stars over a foaming sea. Father in pipe smoke behind his newspaper, red poinsettias out the window. Fifty-five years later, brown spots freckle my hand. My hair is thin, so are my clothes. The world looks through me.

Tokyo-Bangkok. We change airlines. The girls have warmer skin, smiles that soothe me with a mental massage. The result: I'm sweeter, more relaxed. They pour champagne, I raise the glass over dancing whitecaps five miles below. Sky and sea in perfect nuptial, bopping in spangled moondance to Thelonious Monk on the jazz channel. "Blues Five Spot." Johnny Griffin, tenor sax, Roy Haynes, drums. Appropriate, given part of a poem by Ira Cohen that I pasted in my journal before leaving home:

HOMAGE TO MONK

You outdid the
rain at its own
    game...

Turning in your
        own
circle you wore
your music like
    a hat.......

Under which I respond, evermore tipsy with drink:

You made
Just a Gigolo
    Misterioso...
through
Ugly Beauty, your hat
    kept you on.......

A new continent slips under the fuselage. Lights dot Vietnam. Lights dot Cambodia. Lights grow in magnitude and complexity in Thailand. After so many hours up, we come down. Engines whine, wings tilt, flaps unroll. Piercing the clouds, we draw a large circle, touch wet tarmac. Moving with the light of speed from one continent to another, how long will it take to decompress, find new rhythm, become pedestrian again?

Our first steps, beyond fresh papaya salad and Asian coffee, are to Wat Pho's reclining Buddha. Somnolent, wide awake, smiling between dreams, this Buddha, like so many others, lets me remember how I was before I looked. In this 19th-century chapel, we join Thai pilgrims, drop tiny coins into 108 good-luck bowls as we round his mother-of-pearl feet, head of gold curls shaped like conch shells. One hundred eight, so pervasive in Buddhism—did it arise from a sage observing the fine hairs of a caterpillar in the rising sun? And then to mathematics, philosophy, the dharma wheel's radiating spokes? One hundred eight lines of force supposedly converge in the heart chakra. But who's seen them? Sanskrit, into which Buddha's teachings were first recorded, has 54 letters, each with two male/female counterparts. Hindus say 108 delusions confound the human world. Hindu deities are called by 108 names. And, who knows, Brahma may have cleaned 108 shoestrings from his teeth after tasting the soup of creation.

Wat Pho, called Wat Phra Chetuphon by the Thais, is in the old city, just a skip from the Chao Phraya with its whistling river ferries, barges, and bubbling tugs. It's always touristed, but an early visit before buses arrive to dump their loads, makes it special. It's Bangkok's oldest temple, founded and expanded about the time Bashō was wandering, though you wouldn't know it. The place was entirely remodeled in the 19th century. The reclining Buddha was added, the grounds converted into a university. There were chapels for meditation, gardens for solitude, and pavilions for the study of history, philosophy, astrology, acupuncture, mathematics, and the occult. One can roam for hours here, discover little dead ends where a soothsayer with knotted hair unrolls paper scrolls from crystal weights; where shiny marble lingams are tied with carved wooden phalluses; where porcelain pilgrims ascend miniature mountains, and real ones places flowers and ceramic elephants before a wide-eyed goddess, incense smoking between her toes.

Across from Wat Pho is a massage school with airy pavilions of giant proportions, high ceilings hung with black fans wafting talc and incense through the rooms. Students and teachers are at work on clients, or softly padding between waiting customers bearing trays of towels, oils, medicinal balms. A massage here might be regarded as a good shortcut (no drugs or backbreaking zazen) into the visionary realm of stars and sparks. Deep-tissue eyeball-jolting body work where a Thai woman uses every part of her body (knees, knuckles, elbows, and feet especially) to open up every part of yours. Tissues are kneaded, muscles pounded, bones crack, ears ring with heat, jetlag breaks into minute diagrams of super reality. An erotic kind of pain. Visionary explosions. You begin with a cup of chrysanthemum tea, and end, after the torso is dusted with herbs, with the masseuse's folded palms giving you a xylophone-like rap along shoulders and spine. For $5 each we hand ourselves over for an hour, side by side on a clean white futon, and let the girls begin their work. Across the aisle, a trance-eyed man gets up, rotates his neck, takes a few bills from his wallet, and ambles to the cash counter:

> noon heat
> the masseuse fans herself
> with her client's tip.

We'll further adjust the torso and crack the chakras with a spicy meal in Little India, a brief walk through alleys packed with beady-eyed shoppers wedged among tailors, scribes, eyedrop peddlers, money changers, kids selling cinnamon curls from upside-down sunhats. Merchants unfold tarps, plug in megaphones, slurp milk tea from saucers—and go about arranging three-piece rayon suits, satin thongs, hernia trusses, spring-wire bras, metallic wigs, gold tiaras, plastic third-eyes, and paper thunderbolts. Here you can buy battery-powered emeralds, aluminum tridents, sequined wedding dresses, all-purpose aphrodisiacs, bubble-lamp Baby Krishnas. There are blazing saris draped on deadpan mannequins, snakes in bottles, Chinese-import Ganeshas, jars of molars, spools of recycled Tidy Tooth dental floss.

A few blocks of this and the head is full tilt. In a side alley, we sit at a marble-topped table, cool off with an iced lassi dashed with salt and rose water, then step into Majaraj Food House for vegetarian thali: a big stainless steel tray arranged with bowls of pickled spices, lentil soup, garlic flatbread, mint chutney, smoked eggplant with fresh herbs, and mouth-cooling raita. We indulge, even manage to save room for a honey-sweetened rice pudding sprinkled with slivered pistachios.

Into the heat and color and crashing accents again. Senses unconstricted, nerve endings twiddling. No judgment, expectation, censoring. We're simply high as if on poppy smoke, and thus inclined toward harmony, destined to the illogical, at perfect odds with the majority—yet feeling the urge to make love with everyone. Yep, Bangkok. Over the line, out of the parenthesis. I once asked a friend why he came here. Wide-eyed, with an air of madness, he replied: "Because it's got the JUICE!"

The city, of course, isn't without fault. It breathes spooky sins and mal intent just like any other. There are festering slums, tin-roof migrant shanties, barebone highrise, fart-sick air pollution, deafening noise, idiotic traffic snarl, glamorous sin parlors, shipwrecked orphans, knife-throat racketeers. But there is life, surprise, surreal vibrancy, dangerous pleasure, head-banging bewilderment, people diversity, appetizer overload, unbelievably sweet pineapple, and mangoes that induce orgasmic rapture. As a sign over a beauty parlor near Hotel Privacy puts it:

> FULL HEAD
> MESSAGE
> NO WAITING

## 10 NOVEMBER: BANGKOK

> Sign upstairs:
> SLEEPING PEOPLE
> WALK SOFTLY

A baby lizard showers with me. Parrot out window screams *Awww whaddayawant Awww whaddayawant Awww whaddayawant.* Through white curtains, open sewer smell. Between cats in heat, mortar and pestle grind. Basil, peppercorn, sataw beans in ladder-like pods. Hair cream, toe nail polish, whirling pigeons above sun-dried sheets. A tiny silver thong pinned to a green nylon line. Cukes sliced on the diagonal, garlic turning gold in a steel wok. Star anise chopped into Yunnan tea. Jeweled whiteness between the hair of a cleavered coconut. Weather forecast: "Fog down low. Cold in mountain tops. All other parts hot."

Sign downstairs:
OUTSIDE PEOPLE
CANNOT GO UP STAIR

Fresh fruit, black coffee, toasted baguette, *Bangkok Post* open before me. The world manifest as is, sans imagination. Headlines a kind of weight-loss program for the hungry. The news is okay, but I love the waiter's ability to describe how to eat from a banana leaf, the exact ingredients in a curry, the life of a saltwater snail, the ability of a bell to remain quiet while the sky rings. Nevertheless I peruse the strong-smelling ink, reports of unrest in southern Thailand, where Muslims form the majority.

Back home these protests are given a definite spin, linking them to al Qaeda. Here, they are regarded as a local problem. Cultural, linguistic, and geographic identity of southern Muslims has always set them apart from the rest of Thailand. In provinces where they form a majority, their exclusion from government positions is an affront. On October 25, during a peaceful demonstration in Tak Bai, Narathiwat, 85 people were killed by the military, who violently dispersed 3000 unarmed marchers, using tear gas and guns. Seven protesters were killed on the spot; 78 were crushed and suffocated to death, piled in layers in military trucks en route to detention facilities.

The troops were called in by Thailand's overreactive prime minister, Thaksin Shinawatra, a proclaimed Buddhist from Chang Mai Province, who graduated from a Texas university with a Ph.D. in criminal justice. He's been criticized for his violent war on drugs, his intolerance of criticism, his suppression of journalists who complain of having to give a positive spin to his policies (in January, he was forced to admit that he kept secret a bird-flu outbreak). He's also one of Southeast Asia's wealthiest men, a friend of big business who rules with the air of a CEO.

We'd thought about visiting the deep south, but this puts a damper on things. We don't want to be caught in local crossfire or be mistaken for foreign investors (no matter how scruffy we look) eager to usurp the local economy. Meanwhile, the paper's op-ed page is filled with letters from academics who will meet with the prime minister to discuss peaceful alternatives to the unrest. Don't narrow Muslims into the "enemy" category; declare the three southern provinces an autonomous cultural zone based on religious, linguistic, cultural differences; stop filling local government positions with outsiders; correct misunderstandings of why Thai troops were sent to Iraq, i.e., they went for humanitarian missions—medical aid, road repair, rebuilding schools and mosques. Not to help the U.S. army.

## 11 NOVEMBER: BANGKOK TO SAWANKHALOK

We leave Hualamphong train station on the Sawankhalok Sprinter at exactly 9:30, heading through warm morning sun north, past the ruins of Lopburi, through flat, fertile Chao Phraya river basin. First time either of us has ridden a train to the end of the line. In this case, 500 kilometers, seven hours north of Bangkok to a spur angling west off the main rail. We'll end in Sawankhalok, a river town we don't know much about, save that it has the nearest lodging to the 13th-century ruins of Si Satchanalai, a site much less touristed than nearby Sukhothai, which we've already seen.

The train cuts through the central heartland, with only two stops. Black-shouldered kites and marsh harriers glide over rice paddies. Herons and comb ducks feed in the wetlands. An occasional rise, between stands of palms and bamboo, is planted with orchards. There are greenhouses, too, growing the famous orchids that Thailand exports all over the world. Our map shows the heartland ending just before Si Satchanalai. From there begins the hill country, cooler and higher, and with it the old Lanna kingdom, a region which retains distinct cultural, gastronomic, and architectural pride, its geography linked with that of Laos, Yunnan, and Burma.

Our ride is smooth and relaxing, coaches clean, the friendly porters always sweeping and serving. Only four other farangs are aboard, but they get off early at Phitsanulok. I resume with the *Bangkok Post*—drawn to the usual idiosyncratic tidbits between ongoing splices of the American occupation of Iraq.

### SUMATRAN BRIDGE UNDER THREAT

A landmark bridge in Palembang may collapse because too many people are fond of urinating on its steel pillars. The bridge now leans on an angle and rocks when traffic is heavy. The public works department reports that the bridge had deteriorated because support piers have been weakened by the acidic content of urine whose corrosive forces could spell the eventual collapse of the bridge. In an effort to mend the problem, city officials said cargo vehicles weighing more than one tonne will be diverted from the bridge.

Interesting that officials diverted traffic instead of banning citizens from peeing on the bridge . . .

Another article is accompanied by a photo of a stunning beauty queen receiving congratulatory kisses from two runners up:

## THAI WINS 1ST GLOBAL TRANSVESTITE PAGEANT

Blessed with flawless skin and a flashing smile, Thai college student Treechada Petcharat beat 23 challengers to win the world's first international transvestite beauty pageant. The 19-year-old cross-dresser, looking for all the world like the woman her birth certificate refutes, was crowned Miss International Queen in Pattaya yesterday, beating transvestites and transsexuals from 10 Asian countries, France, and Germany. After showing off his figure in swimwear, an evening gown, and national costume, the student emerged triumphant, richer by US $7000, and with a tiara for his well-coiffured hair. Thailand now awaits next month's staging of the Miss Air Hostess pageant.

It is always a relief to be in a country with a relaxed attitude toward sex. To be far from the prudes, politicians, and clergymen back home, the professional taboo-makers who are unable to loosen their jaws and come out from under their moral standards. Better to walk naked, take to task the obscenity of war, the immoral chaos brought on by the perennial ineptitude of egomaniacs like our preemptive born-again, who murders people in order to liberate them. A British medical journal reports at least 100,000 Iraqis have been killed in Bush's war, with 10,000 U.S. soldiers wounded, another 1500 dead, plus thousands more returning home psychologically maimed. And Rumsfeld smirks: "Stuff happens."

By the time we switch onto the track heading west, the afternoon sun has broken from the sky and filled the trees. It filters through orchards and thick-leafed deciduous spreading over morning-gloried teak houses on stilts, clay water jars underneath their eaves. Little gardens of herbs and taro nestle between split bamboo woven into delicate fences. Sawankhalok, as we arrive, looks tolerably small, walkable. It's on the Yom River, which is hidden behind all the modern concrete buildings. The quaint wooden railroad station, a lovely remnant of another era, is unfortunately engulfed by the new stuff. Many old wooden shophouses do remain, though, in quiet alleys behind the slapdash. Little English is spoken, but with the aid of our phrase book, and a retired teacher eager to practice English (outfitted in a bare-shouldered leopard skin dress), we find an adequate, inexpensive hotel. After a shower, we head into the streets.

The evening market is underway, always a treat in a small Thai town. Mingle with the stream, get lost in the current. Lively street stalls have been set up in the normally sedate business district, with its predictable pharmacy, hardware store, beauty parlor, veterinary supply, and small-engine repair shop. Brightly painted carts with propane burners are ringed with tables and chairs under strings of electric bulbs.

Each table is set with bowls of sliced limes, chili in vinegar, nam pla prik (fish sauce), nam jim satay (a crushed-peanut coconut-milk curry paste). Many of the cooks are husband and wife teams. They take their work seriously, but not without jovial flair. The kids wipe tables, serve water, bring on the food. The elders chop, shred, stir, flash fry. Several vendors grill Yom River fish dashed with lemon and chile; or turn marinated sausage on skewers over bins of charcoal.

Here you can choose fish cakes, fried tofu, bok choy, steaming bowls of noodles with crispy bean sprouts and dipping sauce. Or hot-sour shrimp soup spiced with galangal, lime leaves, lemon grass, garlic, black chile paste, mushrooms, and shallots. Everything's spanking fresh, tasty. We sample, eat, continue to sample, and never feel full as with so many wheat, cheese, bread, pasta, and heavy dessert meals at home. Southeast Asian fare is light. It invigorates the senses, cleans the palate, leaves the mind alert:

> for an appetizer
> a boy opens his mouth
> to the rain.

We sample roasted taro, then sit down for soup and noodles served by a mom/daughter duo with that sweet, respectful, accommodating manner so inherent to the Thais. It's the everyday embodiment of right thought, gentle action; honoring the Buddha in one another; reflecting rather than reacting—behavior that flows, according to the Thais, from a "cool heart." No harsh public outbursts, no arrogant displays of anger or annoyance. A healthy attitude that makes, as Burning Spear says, "social living the best." Perhaps Confucian ethics mixed with Buddhist precepts and the extended-family tradition is what influences this attitude. Everyone living under one roof demands compromise, mutual aid, respect. It's what's missing in America. So many children, parents, grandparents living apart from one another. In America privacy is supposed to insure harmony.

Crowds. Numbers. Amassment. Conglomeration. There is something about what Baudelaire calls "Number" that will always draw me into the crowd. From my first Andean fiestas in Ecuador—the frenzy, the mad whirl, collective rise of the psyche through altered-state mutual consciousness, alcohol, masks, pyrotechnics, etc.—to the multitudes of pilgrims bathing in the Ganges in Varanasi, to the markets of Chichicastenango, Sapa, Cusco, and Xijiang, I've found that "the pleasure of being in crowds is a mysterious expression of sensual joy in the multiplication of Number. *All* is Number. Number is in all. Number is in the individual. Ecstasy is a Number" (Charles Baudelaire: *Intimate Journals*).

The market winds down. Cooks fold up their stands; helpers begin scrubbing woks and pans. Leaving the bazaar, we buy toothpaste, shampoo, a pair of trousers, and flip-flops printed with Che Guevara's face (no problem finding *these* when temple keepers ask that footwear be left in piles on the steps!). Off to the hotel now, where I'll likely fill my notebook using the bathroom as an office (the commode for a chair), where the bulb is bright and won't disturb my beloved's sleep; there's a handy little counter for my colored pencils and ink, too. Behind the market's hubbub, Renée notices an insurance agency whose boldly

lettered sign announces: LIFE ASSURANCE.—Guess you pay a
monthly premium to have someone say you're okay:

> old teeth
> aged wine, my heart
> has a murmur.

## 13 NOVEMBER: SAWANKHALOK TO SI SATCHANALAI

We leave Sawankhalok for Si Satchanalai, 20 kilometers north, an
easy ride on a local bus, with plenty of time to think. Left the guide
book in our hotel room, no matter. Better to simply be present at the
ruins and see what happens, no Lonely Planet or Rough Guide telling
us what not to miss or what means what.

More often on a journey, it's not what you're supposed to be looking
at, or for, but what's on the periphery that's of interest. Much can escape
the eye while focusing on the obvious, looking for meaning, constructing
the events of history, or just plain rambling around in the personal,
emotional sphere. When it comes to poetry, nature, and journeying, I
look to Issa and Bashō, those poet wanderers of old Japan. Or to ancient
China: the more sedentary poets Hsieh Ling-yün, Po Chü-i, Su Tung-
p'o. For a modern sojourner, who can beat the insightful ambling of
Norman Lewis? These are travelers who encourage us toward the less
obvious within the obvious.

Motion is a great catalyst. It sets the head wheeling. I love to scribble
while walking, jot dashboard notes on eight-cylinder auto pilot, let

mind slip into high gear with bus wheels churning. Thoughts are driven deeper into the night to the clack of train wheels (Gershwin wrote most of "Rhapsody in Blue" on a train). Randomly spliced stanzas splatter from the pen while crossing the symbolic salt-water straits by ferry. When the traveling's done, it's always great to return home. Grind French roast, ponder, circle the rooms, empty trash, go out and turn the garden, come in, open a can of olives, crush some garlic, squeeze a lemon, throw oregano and feta into a Greek salad, eat, make the unmade bed, wash dishes, sharpen pencils, circle the desk, books, loose reels of typewriter ink, the whole idea of writing! Whenever it hits me that I'm finally ready, I strap myself into the chair. Make an effort. Clear debris. Slash and burn. Jump into road-trip journal, page by page transcribe scribbles. Pick-axe work. Grind away—Fats Navarro or Mozart or TexMex drifting distantly up from downstairs. If it's spring, the weather can be tumultuous:

> an unexpected gust
> fans the pages into
> new order.

Aswirl in the teeth of darkness, I make no attempt to see straight. Meadowlark sings from a post. Towhee answers from under the lilac. Crow flaps by and caws to its partner. A slice, a snippet, a particle floating inside Saturn's ring, a thread pulling me backward into Eve's cave. Fumble, overturn, backpaddle in whitewater. Ride the undertow, hit head on heaven's door, step into fog on Quandary Peak. Empty water from leaking boots, dive into calligraphic explosions. Within the greater text of the journals comes the discovery of little eyeball-jolting, heart-screaming incidents only slightly noted. Whenever I find them, they cause me to flash and expand into an unexpected sphere of surrealism. Such incidents are worth highlighting, while snipping back the huge details of the fabric. In a nutshell: what is it I find in these jottings that I never looked for? What happened that took me out of the journey into the greater journey within?

> pricked by a nettle—
> the sudden face
> of my mother.

## 13 NOVEMBER: SI SATCHANALAI

The bus driver slows to the entrance kiosk. We deboard, pay the 30 baht Historical Monument fee, receive a visitor's pamphlet, rent midget-size bikes, walk them across a shaky cable bridge, and ride the trails between stone spires. The Khmers began work here in the 12th century, a military outpost for their northern territory. Later, in the 13th century, Si Satchanalai was liberated by Thai leaders and developed into a sister city of Sukhothai. Now it's a silent relic overlooking the Yom River, 700 hectares of crumbling temples, lotus-bud stupas, administrative buildings, libraries, and moss-covered collapsed walls. Unlike Sukhothai, it hasn't been extensively restored; there aren't a lot of tourists. Many of the visitors are monks and pilgrims who burn incense at the Buddhas and wrap stone elephants with gold cloth. There are grassy open plazas, but much of the site is shaded, etched against dense woods at the base of a forested hill. We stray from the wooded paths, catch the smells of a nearby village:

hearth smoke
and wisteria; too soon
this journey full circle.

It's a blessing to be here early in the day. Si Satchanalai absorbs the morning light as do other notable stone monuments of Southeast Asia: Angkor Wat, Pagan, Borobudur, Candi Sukuh. Or, in the Americas: Tikal, Palenque, Macchu Picchu. Places of awe where one feels small again, wiggles back into the universe with proper weight and size. Si Satchanalai's walls, terraces, stairways, and spires expand outward and upward before the eye. There is a slow swelling of captured light. Architecture at once solid steams with warm auras, becomes suddenly weightless, evaporative. To visit during the monsoon, or in morning mist, is to watch stone dematerialize into ether, hear silence chime with metallic vibrations. It's not the clink of the builders' hammers, either, as if in some imagined past. It's the zodiac come down to earth. A reverberating collection of energy, as if this architectural cosmogram were a magnet concentrating the sun's power into a diadem. Stone radiates into human consciousness, fills the psychic stream, manifests itself as music. We inhale it, sit and converse with it. We press against it, taste the essential elements of magma inside the rock, water oozing from faces carved into pillars, air feeding lichens that scour Buddha's smile, erase his eyes, burnish his curls. Everything is still, yet it writhes. Form mingles with formlessness. It's a good place for dreaming:

Buddha too
part of this vanishing
world.

It is the hour to wander, release thought, become naked, float up into the spires with dragonflies. A butterfly's shadow whisks the upraised hand of a fear-dispelling Buddha. Water is puddled in a bodhisattva's footprint, an arrow of sun shoots from it. Broken serpents, cracked angels, missing deities. An empty niche returns my voice. Who graced this darkness? Whose atoms continue to disappear and recombine into pollen, chaff, sap? A passing cloud nibbles at the Temple of the Golden Mountain. A tail of rain beads empty space. I meditate while strolling, lean against a stone lotus:

> in a clearing of silence
> a name I cannot pronounce
> surrounds me.

## 14 NOVEMBER: SAWANKHALOK TO PHRAE

Bright red bus decorated with flowers and plastic amulets. Falsetto voice undulates through torn speaker. The driver is tiny behind his huge bandaged steering wheel. The passengers are animated in spheres of talk or aloof in quiet contemplation. Geese are aboard. Purple stalks of sugar cane. Bags of grain. Coils of rope. Clanking bottles of fish sauce. Pigs under a blanket. Fringe from the ceiling. Little fans attached with streamers. I am all child and smiles for the two-hour ride north to the town of Phrae.

Yesterday we visited the Sawankhalok museum outside of town over the Yom River. No other visitors, and the staff, eager to please, seemed happy we were there. The holdings were in excellent shape, well displayed: ceramic Buddhas, celadon bowls, glazed plates, jars, pitchers, zoomorphic figurines. Surf green, burnt umber, and buttermilk were the prominent colors. Some pieces were excavated from the kilns of Si Satachanalai, others retrieved from a sunken ship in the Gulf of Thailand.

Potters who worked in Si Satchanalai in the 14th and 15th centuries were among the finest in Southeast Asia. When China's Ming Dynasty collapsed, its ceramics production went with it. Thailand filled the market. Sukothai increased output in Si Satchanalai, shipped the goods to Vietnam, the Philippines, and Indonesia. Among the museum's displays of stoneware, celadon, and incised ceramics, our favorites were bowls etched with spiraling fish. There were curious hunchback figures, too. We bought some miniature glazed horses, turtles, bulls, and rabbits—replicas of the old stuff—and two bowls decorated with fish and flowers. Heavy items to carry at the start of a month-long trip!

Over the hills towards Phrae, we cross into the north country. The feeling is more intimate, the roads wind and tuck into the hills. Here and there the rice harvest is in progress. Cutting, threshing, winnowing, all by hand. Every nook and cleft of tillable land between the forested hills is a checkerboard of bronze and emerald. Rice in various stages. Ready-to-be-cut gold against still-ripening green. Where the grain is ready for harvest, plastic bags flutter on bamboo poles to keep away the birds. Men and women, with scarves over faces to keep dust and chaff away, bend with sickles, swipe and cut in long graceful harmony. As they go, they gently lay the stalks in their wake. In some areas barefoot farmers trod behind huge water buffaloes, loosening the soil with wooden plows. Heavy beams are dragged over the ground to flatten the clods, firming a bed for the transplanting of baby rice shoots— brought in baskets on heads from seed beds protected by nets. The seedlings are set into the mud in precisely even rows. The land isn't steep enough to be terraced here, but in the far north you can climb high and stand above sculpted mountains, gazing down into a dazzle of wet mirrors. Sun and clouds ricochet into the eye. Songs of frogs and rice planters carry upward into the ear. I cannot help recalling Bashō traveling the deep interior of Japan in 1689:

> the beginning of poetry
> a rice planting song
> in the back country.

To travel is to open a door to another room in the house to see who's there. I wish we were all on good terms in this floating world. Passing these fields of sun and song, everything sparkles. The idea of afterworld, heaven, immortality, seems far-fetched. What's wrong with paradise now, ourselves evaporative on the diamond leaf? Quarrels, wars, pure futility! Load up the planes, strap a bomb to your belt, stop dead the harvest, the work of the family. The more we fight, the meaner we get. Christian crusades. Muslim jihad. Doomsday drop kick. Pride of power. Triflers, preachers. Lovers of doctrine, haters of doubt, mystery, crooked lines. Religion, a shock to my system. As a boy I was a fire worshiper, climbed trees to get closer to the sun. Stood on water, let waves of light ride me to shore. Sat in mother's chair drawing thick-lead topo squiggles on newsprint. Salt water sea grottoes, zigzag bear trails, granite domes catching solar rays bounced from iced-tarn cirques. Pantheism! All things me as I am they. Mundo erecto. Sweat running upside down on my face, arms to the earth, hanging from elm limb, listening to mockingbirds, inhaling dry camphor of eucalyptus. Brown dust on guavas. Dried persimmons—wafer-thin Eucharists—melting on my tongue. Holy eternity in each bending blade of fennel. Childhood! They hoped I'd become a priest, but I wanted to be a test pilot, an actor, a ventriloquist. From my bedroom I could see the lights of Universal, Disney, Warner Brothers. As I went to sleep, movie stars said their lines, men pulled into place painted clouds, plywood cities. Illusion slowly became a familiar guest.

> between
> flashing sickles
> a temple bell sounds.

## 14 NOVEMBER: PHRAE

Phrae is bigger than we expected. All these places are. Still, it's a town, and one that seems to cater mostly to its own citizens, visiting Thai families, a stray businessman. As for foreigners, hardly a one. *Conde Nast* hasn't written it up, so prices are cheap: 200 baht, $5, for a hotel with private bath, hot water, soap, towels, writing desk, and big teak closets (no wonder we've seen so much teak reforestation en route). Nights are cooler here, so an overhead fan is sufficient. Phrae's market is handy, too, right around the corner from where we lodge. To boot, everybody's very friendly.

Today, after rambling and losing our way, we ducked into a tailor's shop. I rehearsed a few lines of Thai, hoping to get some directions, but the owner, a dark and handsome Indian gentleman in his mid-forties, surprised us by speaking perfect English. He had moved here decades ago with his parents, married a Thai woman, started a branch of the family business. His father owned another store near the night market. "You'll see him in a purple turban sitting out front. Loves to talk." Then he showed us the way back to our hotel, the Maeyom Palace—which we call the Mayhem Palace. "And your name?" I asked. "Kaka. Just call me Kaka."

The old part of town is not quite what we expect, but it's our own fault. We always think we're going to find something belonging to some earlier era. According to the guide book: "Phrae, the teak industry's center in the 19th century, boasts the largest concentration of teak houses in Thailand, all of them to be found inside the old city walls. If you're a fan of traditional teak architecture, there's more here than in any other similar-sized city in Thailand." We imagine the new concrete town stopping point blank where high, whitewashed walls keep development at bay, the 21st century locked out. Inside those magic walls, we fantasize ambling among slow-moving pedestrians in narrow alleys full of wooden temples and homes, looms clacking, plenty of bicycles, no televisions. But it's not quite so. The new city merges with the old, the ancient walls have largely melted into dust, sky is filled with TV aerials, monks sit around boom boxes. Lots of Toyota pickups, no bicycles. Plenty of polyester, no looms.

It's always difficult to come to grips with how the world has changed, how every place is becoming the same, lives cloned by television and corporate advertising, politics dogging trade, overpopulation and mass migration adding crowded slums to cities and towns, people running from political threats, war, draught, environmental rape, military and corporate confiscated lands. In 1960 the world population was three billion; it's now over six. Because so much of the population is lumped together in cities, corporate oligarchies can all the more easily go about their aggressive "let's make the world all the same" policies, grinding the pillars of culture into dust heaps to be remolded into identical building blocks. Stamp out diversity! That's their motto. It's a threat to global autocracy. Monoculture best serves the needs of corporate dictators. Homogenization, full steam ahead! Burger King in Kunming, McDonald's in Chang Mai, Wal-Mart in Teotihuacán. Gringos pulverizing the Spaniards who pounded the Aztecs who taxed and sacrificed the tribes after the collapse of the Toltecs. Now it's the conglomerate robot, with elite representatives from multi-continent think tanks, damming rivers, remaking landscapes, designing them around military zones, confiscated wildlands, pipelines, freeways, airports, industrial centers. Everywhere, everybody's brainwashed with a single idea of what life is, who they need to be, what they need (to buy) to live that life.

In 1992, Eduardo Galeano, in his chronicles *We Say No*, wrote:

"In the era of 'national security,' people live imprisoned so that business may live free, and the cultural industry consolidates an alliance with the military apparatus. With few exceptions, the mass media spreads a colonist and alienating culture, designed to justify the unequal organization of the world . . . They falsify the past, lie about reality, and propose a model of life that exalts crime as a heroic feat, lack of scruple as a virtue, and egotism as an inherent need. They teach competition, not sharing. In the world that they set forth, people belong to automobiles and culture is consumed, like a drug; but is not created. This is also a culture, a culture of resignation, that generates artificial needs to obscure real ones."

Ten years later, in *Upside Down*, he culled these statistics:

> "There are 1.2 billion TV sets in the world. Recent surveys in the Americas, from north to south, reveal the omnipresence and omnipotence of the small screen:—in four out of 10 homes in Canada, parents are unable to recall a single family meal eaten without the TV on—tied to the electronic leash, children in the United States spend 40 times as many hours watching TV as talking to their parents—in most homes in Mexico, the furniture is arranged around the television—in Brazil one-fourth of the population admits they would not know what to do with their lives if television did not exist. Working, sleeping, and watching television are the three activities that eat up most of people's time in today's world, something politicians are well aware of. This electronic network, which brings the pulpit into millions and millions of homes, delivers an audience bigger than any ever dreamed of by the many preachers the world has produced."

I am thinking of a visit to Bali, early 1990s:

> pavilions once reserved
> for storytellers now lit
> with sitcoms.

Late afternoon, the heat suddenly heavy. We're at the end of our walk through the old part of town, which has proved rewarding after all. Many intact teak houses bordering quiet lanes. Burmese-Lao influenced temples. A 13th-century wat filled with people making floats for an upcoming festival. Women crosslegged on a cool verandah opposite the wat, laughing and gossiping, folding paper into tubes, plaiting leaves, arranging flowers. Suddenly, out of nowhere, a smiling man opens two folding chairs, places them under a shade tree, gestures for us to sit and enjoy the temple's beauty. Ringside seats! He brings two glasses of Coca Cola and a third of ice. The bright gold facade shimmers in the sun while we cool off. Among the carved and gilded vines, apsaras, and figures from the *Ramayana*, Hanuman spins inside a braided wheel, looking playfully fierce. And there beneath him:

> after meditation
> monks gathered around
> their boom box.

## 15 NOVEMBER: PHRAE

Ladders, drums, huge cast-iron bells in temple courtyards capture our attention. They're usually in small pavilions, protected from sun and rain under canopies of painted beams covered with wood shingles or tile. The ladder symbolizes higher striving, exit from earthly realm into dream flight. It's how the shaman steps into the supernatural. The bell and drum induce body and mind into super-consciousness. They set up vibrations that cleanse and quiet the psyche, beckon us into a higher sphere. Good reminders, in this confusing world, that ritual is necessary to call the spirit away from distraction. The bells are silent unless I strike them, and I occasionally do. They have enormous presence, resonance that replicates the dynamic forces that reverberate through the universe. Humans, too, add to the reverberation. With their voices, commands, bombs, slander, incense, songs, prayers, they bring irreversible effect into the entire life system—transforming, altering, destroying, occasionally rejuvenating.

Jack Kerouac's *The Scripture of Golden Eternity* is a good, thin book to journey with (it could have been written in Thailand). In one passage he becomes what he calls "the golden eternity in mortal animate form." As a poet and loner, he often transcended that form, lifting out of his body, beyond earthly phenomena. Once, while witnessing "the Clear Sight of Varied Crystal Shining Mountains shifting in the Air," he grappled with words (in *Green Pome*) to describe the experience:

                "Shattered
                        Brilliant
                Transcendental
                        Hammered."

We walk out to Ban Wangburi, an exceptionally preserved gingerbread mansion built between 1906 and 1909 by Cantonese craftsman for the last prince of Phrae. Unfortunately, it's closed for the weekend, but at least we can walk around it, look up into three stories of wooden filigree trellis work, countless shuttered windows, an array of carved wooden screens almost Islamic in design. The original pink and white paintwork has been maintained and the grounds are shrubbed and cool, somewhat British in feel, a bit too trimmed for my taste. Returning to our hotel, Renée discovers a woman who's nodded off on the table of her sewing machine. She had been sewing a bright orange monk's robe. "My mother," says her daughter who tends the ice-cream stand next door, "works hard. 73. Still more to do."

                        asleep on her arm
                        in the middle of a stitch
                        —the seamstress.

Wat Prabat Ming is a modern wat overshadowing the older, more attractive buildings in its compound. We watch a crowd of people getting ready to enter the meditation hall. Beforehand, they make purchases of cellophane-wrapped bundles of incense, soap, flowers, toothpaste, matches, toilet paper, candles, cups, dishes, and assorted fruit. A young man waves us aside and tells us that these people are pilgrims who will tie the offerings, along with new robes, to parasols and present them to monks who will offer prayers to the ancestors. "It's called thot kathin, a merit-making ceremony." The man is a bank clerk, glad for the excuse to practice his English. He gives us each a souvenir coin and a Thai postage stamp. Another sweet moment with a complete stranger.

After sunset, we search for green papaya salad at the night market. None to be found. Seems to be more of an afternoon treat to be washed down with a cold Singha beer in the heat. There's a fine assortment of cheap curries in the stalls, and we peruse them. After a round of inspection, we choose an eatery, take a seat, share a large helping of steamed jasmine rice, green curry with chicken, bamboo shoots, basil, lemongrass, aromatic lime leaf, and yellow curry with pork and red peppers. The yellow is gaeng hang lay, of Burmese influence. Its flavor is milder than the green, more earthy. It's spiced with ginger, tamarind, and turmeric. The latter, a cousin of ginger, gives the distinctive color. A pitcher of water is served, all smiles. Afterwards, at another stand, we sample a delicious helping of Chinese pot stickers with soy-garlic dipping sauce. We wander a bit, go back for more pot stickers, then treat ourselves to soymilk with jujubes (tapioca balls), a drink found in "bubble tea" lounges popular with young Asians in cities back home. Renée orders it hot; I order it cold. Each drink comes with a glass of light, palate-cleansing tea. We end the night with a rice-flour crepe toasted on an iron griddle, folded into a cone, sweets and shredded egg yoke inside.

Leaving the market, we notice how ingeniously each food stand advertises its specialty, either with Thai script gracefully calligraphed on chalkboards, or with the featured foods hung from awning wires. One cart displays strands of cured pork between coils of handmade noodles and sheaves of fresh bok choy. On the way to our hotel, we pass a Chinese shrine, pillars decorated with clouds and waves, serpents with mirrors for scales, electric bulbs for eyes. Women, wearing bright red aprons over lime-green dresses, sell whole roasted duck, tangerines, dragon fruit, mung bean cakes, Yunnan apples, and donuts. Nearby is Kaka's father, unmistakable in his purple Punjabi turban, perched on a stool in front of his tailory. Alert, well traveled, he speaks four languages. "I'm 86 years old, free of responsibility. That's why I am healthy. I've got nowhere to go, except . ." and he trails off, pointing skyward, a copper amulet dangling from his wrist. Then adds: "At age 60 I decided to leave India, go someplace small, retire into my real life. I needed quiet."

It occurs to me that's exactly what I did at almost the same age, though I hardly think of myself as being retired. Never had a job. Besides, to retire into quiet is to take on the work of solitude. Almost to the hotel, there's yet another tall chimney jutting from the ubiquitous temple crematory:

> old age—
> he begins to notice
> every cremation tower.

## 16 NOVEMBER: PHRAE TO NAN

Renée learns that we failed to visit one of the more spectacular wooden temples of Phrae, but too late. We're rattling along on a bus over the hills, into Nan Province. The temple was Wat Chom Sawan, Monastery of the Highest Heaven, "finest Burmese wat in the north," says the guidebook, "one of the purest surviving Shan monasteries in Lanna." On the map I see that it's outside the old city walls, probably why we missed it. Or, in haste, maybe I confused it with the teak mansion, Ban Wangburi. Photos of Chom Sawan show a series of delicate, interlocking teakwood pavilions with multi-tiered pagodas. The interior is supposed to be filled with Buddha imagery, gilded wickerwork, and scriptures painted on wafer-thin ivory.

Words painted on ivory! The image conjures up lamaseries in Ladakh, where I first saw Buddhist prayer books shelved in wooden slots above meditation benches covered with Tibetan rugs. Not books in the Western sense, but lengths of thick handmade paper calligraphed with mantras, gathered between painted wood covers, and wrapped in silk. Years later, in Bali, I would find verses of the Ramayana scrimshawed on palm leaves gathered in the same manner, unbound, between decorated covers.

Bus wheels turn beneath me; so do the ones in my head. I see myself, a youngster in college, and the poet Jack Hirschman—shoes untied, hair afire, ink between his fingers—waving before me his experimental poem "Interchange." He wants me to design and print it as a book, not an ordinary book, either. The poem, inspired by Mallarme's

"A Throw of the Dice," is dedicated to John Cage, and he envisions the text broken up and printed on squares of thick paper, black on white, then put into a box in no particular order (he's secured 300 blank 7"x7" magnetic tape boxes, onto which I'll silk-screen the title). Taken from the box, the poem can be read spontaneously, the "pages" passed around to an audience.

I completed "Interchange" in 1964. It was exhibited on a wall at Zora Gallery, Los Angeles. The black-on-white pages surrounded a white-on-black axis page. Jack read from it, plucking words like stars from a constellation. I was transfixed! The entire experience took the lid off my head. Jack had changed my concept of the book (and of poetry) forever. A concept that was to be reinforced during travels throughout Asia in upcoming decades.

## 17 NOVEMBER: NAN

Our spotless, airy guest house in Nan has shiny wooden floors and windows opening through leafy trees to a quiet neighborhood with sois almost too narrow for automobiles. Lack of American names in the guest book reveals how many Americans are hesitant to leave their country and travel. Paranoia has increased. People's fear of the lurking "terrorist" has tweaked their minds to the point where staying home isn't a bad option at all: soaking up more propaganda from the Bush machine, lolling about in the rocking boat of internal homogenization, passively imagining a world beyond—or actively dismissing it.

During the McCarthy era, it was the manipulative Cold-War fear of the Commies. Reds coming at us from everywhere: in movies, on stage, over the air, through the window. In Southern California, the nuns drilled us for earthquakes, and for the Russians. Air-raid practice happened every Thursday, timed perfectly to interrupt our church history class, in which, ironically, we were studying the Holy Land, the Fertile Crescent between the Tigris and Euphrates. "Eden is a real place," explained Sister Mary Esther, "a green triangle between two rivers in the desert. Look, it's right here on the globe." For the first time, a place strong in my imagination as fable had been given a real geographic locale. Meanwhile, the sirens. Under the desk, hold your head, get ready for the bomb! I never was clear who had it, but I'd seen in *Life* that we had one, too, and had actually dropped it. During air raid practice, I secretly hoped something would blow. I wanted disaster to remake my world. I hoped to find myself in the arms of my third-grade love, Consuelo, as falling debris buried us and the Angel took us to heaven. A better scenario, perhaps, than living to be an elder of 60, the hubris of my country shameful, so much of the world around me broke and hobbling.

A Danish teacher working in Nan assures us that a vote against Bush was a vote with the world's majority. "If you feel bad about the election outcome, console yourselves with the realization that you're not only with the one-half of the U.S. that voted against him, you're with the rest of the world who disapprove of him."

Outside, the air is sweet, sunshine bright. A dog limps into a temple gate between two stone griffins, incense burning in their nostrils. Potted spider lilies bank a miniature moat. We find a bench and unwrap sticky rice and coconut from banana leaves:

> muddy pool
> I wait for the lotus
> to open.

Nan is a fairly calm town of about 25,000. Truly north country: blue air, warm days, cool nights. River valley rice fields, lofty hills, Laos next door. The rice grown here, alternating with soy beans, is most likely khao neeo, "sticky rice," a chewy, glutinous long-grain rice with a slightly sweet flavor. To prepare it you soak it overnight, then steam it in a basket until soft. Eaten with fingers, dipped in sauce, paired with a bite of the main course, it's a treat—the daily bread of northern Thailand and Laos. It arrives at your table in a beautiful little bamboo basket. Along the road, on a bike ride, you can buy it from vendors who steam it in bamboo tubes over charcoal fires to give it a smoky flavor.

The Nan Museum, a short walk from our guest house, is the only museum we've ever visited where shoes are removed before entering. It's housed in a teakwood palace built in 1903 for a prince, but it feels more like a princess's dream: very feminine in proportions and detail. Ornate eaves under steep roofs. Tall shuttered windows, narrow and elegant, that open toward the gold stupa of Wat Chang Kam, gleaming through the trees. There's lots of Buddhas here, religious artifacts, sky rockets, exhibits of Nan ethnic groups, ceramics, and exquisite textiles, including the much-prized "water falling, river flowing" design woven by Tai Lü people. There's also a rare oddity: a 40-pound black elephant tusk resting in the arms of an open-winged, red-beaked Garuda. The tusk doesn't interest me, but Garuda does. I've seen him in so many places, always connected with Hindu mythology. This time, however, I see him as the ancient bird upon which seers rode into dream states of terror and ecstasy. One has to claw back beyond all the modern mythologies (even millennia-old Hindu stuff)to get to the bones of it all. In Thailand, Garuda is the king's personal emblem. In Indonesia, the national airline. In Bali, its ghost flies from sparks in the heat of trance dancing.

Outside the museum, small boys are roughing each other on the treed walkway. In a shady corner, picking and plucking things invisible to put in an imaginary purse,

> a little girl
> collects sunlight
> from the shadows.

Wat Phumin, Nan's most revered temple, is one of our favorites. Built in the late 16th century, renovated in the 19th, it has an unusual cruciform chamber covered with sweeping multi-tiered roofs peaked with flame-like wisps. There are four directional portals, each with a tall wooden door intricately carved with floral designs. When we walk through we're in a womb-like chamber. Intimate, majestic, huge, small. A deceptive space. Sanguine, elastic. It brings up a line from the Tao Te Ching: "the perfect square has no corners."

The interior is dim, yet subtly radiant, a warm ember. The space is broken by 12 immense teak pillars, brightly lacquered red, black, and gold. Like trees (which they were), their trunks grow thinner as they disappear toward the ceiling. Each is banded with carved and painted flowers, devas, elephants, and geometric patterns. Within the patterns are tiny mirrors, talismanic reflectors that reverse evil into its own eye and replace it with sunlight. Each sparkling pinpoint is like a miniature pond, the glass in which we first knew our own faces.

Where the 12 pillars meet the ceiling, they support a network of tie beams. Between the beams is a checkerboard of deep-green squares carved with gold star-flowers at their centers. Below is the wat's main attraction: four enormous Laotion-style Buddhas seated back to back. They are brightly gilded, delicately sculpted, their bodies flooded with light from each of the cardinal-direction doorways. The effect is like being at the heart of a spiritual compass, or like being in your own head, light searing in from four eyes to concentrate into a single, golden dazzle.

We slowly walk the interior walls, profuse with murals depicting Buddhist tales, scenes from Buddha's life, and from the daily life of the Thai Lü—Nan's prominent ethnic population who painted the murals, late 19th century. We photograph a few details: a man whispering into the ear of a courtly woman wrapped in a textile of rippling water designs; a bare-breasted woman, arms erotically raised doing her hair into a topknot, her sarong rendered with all the intricate folds of garments seen in Japanese prints. The subtle transparency of the murals—vermilions, blue violets, malachites—call to mind the colors of the Aztec murals at Teotihuacán.

It's hard to explain what it means to visit these Thai temples. For some, the comparison to visiting European cathedrals might suffice. I loved Chartres because it is a true sanctuary. In the darkness, it is the Mother who presides. Surrounded by stained-glass windows, it is the labyrinth that provides the haunting experience of walking the inward-narrowing spiral, retracing the ups and downs of one's life. As in Chartres, you enter a Thai wat, especially the more delicate northern-style ones, to experience sacred space. Dirt, noise, and the chaos of the secular world are left behind. There are architectural details to absorb, sure, but one enters Wat Phumin primarily to leave the world's heat, step into the cool, offer a prayer for the well being of all, a nod in the direction of heaven—which is a nod to mother earth. Bow three times, honor body-mind-spirit, wisdom-insight-compassion. Fold palms to heart, lay them to the earth. Lose the eyes to the inner chiaroscuro, the architecture of the psyche:

> in the darkness
> a sparrow sharpens its beak
> in Buddha's palm.

The big, blazing doors are left open to the rushing city, but the cudgel of jabber and motors and foot-slap beyond the gates is barely audible. What is audible is the ticking of the heart, the monologue of the mind dragging its clanking anchors, the slow fireworks of the soul examining itself, rearranging the body to meet the world again. How far we are from the European cathedral, the beaten prophet on his cross. The Buddha shines. He smiles. He needs no halo. His entire body is radiant. Sometimes he stands, arms raised, hands held at shoulder level, palms turned outward to dispel harm: physical, psychological. Or he sits, legs crossed, eyes closed, breathing slowed, concentrating on the ultimate truth of existence: ignorance, suffering. Sometimes he walks forward, palms emptying, dispersing favors, bestowing compassion—with a Mona Lisa look. Sometimes he brings one hand down, touches the earth, acknowledging his oneness with all sentient beings.

Bend to the Buddha out there, and you bend to the one inside. Sit for a moment and you inevitably rummage through grief, limitations, beliefs, doubts, expectations, failures, quests. The dead, the estranged, the sexual postures so blatantly juicy, are now the anatomy of memory, taught parchment of atrophy. Broken rapture, half-stripped furniture, splashed-melon arguments—who likes everything that floats past the inner eyeball in this silence? But it's comforting to be with this discomfort before a larger-than-life being who smiles, a break from the spooky Padre of Doom hiding behind cloak and wooden screen, strapping youth with guilt, penance, fire, limbo's nerve gas. Screw limbo! At Wat Phumin, Buddha looks on, lips parted with kind understanding. He's here to bestow radiance, elicit the possibility of stepping back into the world with a clear eye. The temple is you, every step you take.

We leave the same way we come in, via the concrete steps bordered with naga balustrades. These undulating mythical serpents (like the ones at Angkor Wat) bring us into the city again—with empty minds. Much later, we discover Michael Freeman's excellent handbook, *Lanna: Thailand's Northern Kingdom,* and learn that Wat Phumin's nagas are sculpted so that they appear to swim through the wat, entering one side, exiting the other, carrying you right into Buddha's lap and out again. Also of interest, the symbolic multiple roofs. Freeman remarks: "The chapel has a five-tier roof, decorated with nagas symbolizing the water flowing down from Mount Meru." Wat Phumin is meant to represent a sacred mountain shedding heavenly rains, slope to slope, feeding the rivers (nagas), which give life to the world.

## 18 NOVEMBER: BAN TOEI

Aloft in the mountains, having traveled 75 kilometers north from Nan, we wake in a floating world. Primitive thatch hut, futon on split-bamboo floor, whole thing up on stilts. Big datura bush under balcony, creamy blossoms dripping like shower heads. Odor of matted leaves and lemongrass. Rain pattering a floppy banana tree. It woke us at midnight, and with it came one of my favorite haikus, by Hakurakutan:

> evening rain
> the bashō speaks
> of it first.

Mists part, ridges and valleys appear, then clouds come again and all disappears. The mountains are not solid, they escape before the eye, slopes half erased, moisture veiling their edges. Coves and wooded edges turn melancholy with mist, then brightly open with sun. A gorge, a cleft, eternity's edge. Po Chü-i would have relished these rain-slick jade crags. Ink wash on idle page, happy deep-stream wandering among wind-ruffled fields. Wish I had the patience to stay awhile, enjoy an archaic conversation with the spirit of this place. I think of Chinese hermit painters, escaping political turmoil (fourth century, and again in war-filled 10th), taking to the hills, planting gardens, writing poetry, studying the Tao, rediscovering their true nature within landscapes like this. Monkeys, birds, woodcutters for companions. Lofty pines fading, bending, reinventing themselves between storms. Pleasant days, too— spring mountains stepping forward between flowering apricots to become guests at the poet's bench.

Renée reminds me of the pitfalls of impatience. Arriving in a place only to be thinking of the next, and the next. Not settling in, not accepting foul weather. But, damn, it's too slippery to do any walking around this high mountain hut. It's chilly and gray. A swig of hot rice wine would boost my spirits (but 7 A.M. is a bit too early!). We'll thumb a ride down the mountain, catch a bus, slowly make way back to Nan, stop at a village or two, peruse some textiles. Besides, food is limited here and I'm getting hungrier by the minute, remembering that sweet little cafe in Nan, coffee trees flowering outside, the owner speaking to us in Thai, correcting my tones, pronunciation, placement of nouns and adjectives. All cheer and smiles, she brings on the pumpkin soup, vegetarian spring rolls, sauteed morning glories, sticky rice, iced coffee. Beauty, graciousness. A hand from a sleeve of moss-green silk, water filling a pottery urn, flies praying on the banister rail:

> misting hills
> seen through rose petals
> blown against the screen.

## 18 NOVEMBER: NONG BUA

Nong Bua is a lean, orderly Tai Lü village just off the highway going north to Laos. The Tai Lü migrated from Yunnan (Xishuangbanna) in the mid-19th century, and are particularly known for their fine weaving. The Lotus Pond Wat is here, too, but the pounding rain limits our exploration. Too bad, because the facade is richly carved with ornate scrollwork framing a gold tiger, Renée's totem. We duck inside, but the murky day provides only fair illumination for the painted murals. They're similar to those of Wat Phumin, but not in great shape. One of the seated Buddha's shoulders is draped with a sash of four-point star flowers, a nice example of Tai Lü weaving, as are the banners with striking geometric designs that hang from the gilded teak ceiling.

When the rain breaks we head into the lanes behind the wat to the weaving co-op. Here we find a textile we've been searching for: an exquisite cotton tapestry woven with a traditional nam lai (flowing-water) design: charcoal, maroon, green, gold, and silver. The nam lai is bordered with eye-dazzling diamonds; when looked at long enough, they reverse themselves into turtles—appropriate fertility symbols to accompany the water. We purchase it, and Renée selects another tapestry, embroidered with starbursts, hearts, diamonds, butterflies, flowers, and peacocks.

On the bus back to Nan, the weather clears, the hills stand out sharply, rising steeply from either side of the road. Newly planted teak trees vigorously seek the sun. Plots of corn, taro, and yams run up and down the clearings. Oranges and tangerines ripen in orchards behind rows of cotton. The stilt houses are clean, well tended, some with freshly spaded gardens of manioc, papayas, and bougainvilleas. One house has a huge spray of bamboo sweeping its eaves, a spirit house (to promote harmony) on a post located in an auspicious corner of the yard. The bare-dirt compound is meticulously swept and completely sparse, save for a big blue watering can and a few fallen leaves. Into this zen-like patio ambles an old man, bare chested, wearing shorts and plastic sandals. He bends to the leaves, and one by one goes about picking them up. Could be me in a few more years. "Already is," Renée laughs. In another compound, lots of housecleaning. Girls whisking a balcony, boys hauling quilts and mattresses out the door. Women in a sunny corner of the yard with paddles and brooms:

> the futon pounders—
> above them, white clouds
> filling with wind.

## 19 NOVEMBER: NAN

Cool, wet shade. Vine-grown open-air cafe. Noodle vats, squid over charcoal, basil on chopping block, fish playing in a bucket underneath. Not long, and the cleaver will be on their heads, and their bodies in ours. We order iced beer, toasted cashews and lime. Followed by a slow feast of lemongrass salad, sticky rice, minced pork with mint, coriander, and cloves. Fresh pineapple for dessert. Peaceful meal, until a foreigner sitting in a far corner, beer bottle in one hand, cigarette in the other, meanders over. A scarecrow of an American ex-pat: tiny darting eyes, shotgun monologue, cell phone in Hmong-embroidered case, ballpoint pens behind the dirty lip of his shirt pocket. Says he's in the process of moving here from southern Thailand where he's managed to piss off a mayor "who's been interrupting my business plans." He smells of nervous sweat, the ends of his hair are split, the underneaths of his nails black. He's full of himself, the deals about to bring him a fortune, the scam he's got going with a Jesuit boys' school that needs a monthly chaperone to accompany students back and forth between Bangkok and Delhi. "And that's me," he lights up another cigarette, blowing smoke into our faces. "It's an easy swing. Made in heaven. I just get 'em to India, stay in a nice hotel, buy a silk suit and write it off as business expense, fly back to Bangkok, stay in another nice hotel, collect my check. The little suckers give me any trouble, I tell 'em 'you misbehave, I'll throw you out on the wing and let you blow off.' Often feel like doing it, too."

Eventually he gets a call, goes into a corner and paces, returns to give us his business card, talking all the while, then (still talking) cocks a wave and hastens off. Good. We can now do a little catch-up in our journals. An act that seems to be noticeably rare among travelers these days. With laptops, internet, and cybercafes, hardly anyone opens a diary anymore. They're fidgeting with electronic screens, scanning messages, playing games, babbling into miniature cellulars which never let them stray from home. Or, it's the deadening flicker of satellite TV, cloned CNN, pirated DVDs.

> travel diary—
> toothpick, leaf, ticket stubs
> for bookmarks.

I was 12 when we got our first TV. I thought it was interesting, but not terribly important. Books were better companions. You could take them to bed, fill your head, put them down, go to sleep with new dreams. The color plates were journeys in themselves. My copy of *A Child's Garden of Verses* was illustrated in Aubrey Beardsley's style, all writhing silhouettes. *Homes and Habits of Wild Animals* had beautiful watercolors: otters sliding down river banks, wolverines busting into a hunter's cabin, grizzlies carrying fish from streams, a mother possum with babies wrapped around her tail. *Famous Paintings* was filled with great art. I didn't care for Van Gogh, but liked the drama in Bellows' *Stag at Sharkies*, and in Homer's *Gulf Stream*. Why El Greco made his figures all rubbery, like people in fun-house mirrors, I couldn't comprehend. Chagall's violin player in the snow with a horse-headed angel floating above didn't seem like a famous painting to me. But Bellini's *Saint Francis in Ecstasy* fit the category perfectly: a hermit who lived in a cave trellised with flowers, his arms inviting the birds, while distant castles floated in the sun. Brown tunic, rope for a belt, bare feet, a book on a makeshift desk among the rocks—my man!

My parents provided me with an early sense of travel, in books and in the car. Breathtaking forays in the old Chevrolet, up the California coast, into the Sierra Nevadas, out into the red-rock desert. Back home, I had my own private table, a box of pencils, stack of newsprint. I was encouraged to write a line or two about places we went: a description, an emotion. And to do some drawings. These drawings and writings were stapled into my first books. For the finishing touch, I was asked to make a cover. It all took place in the cave of delight, a corner of the living room, a ray of sun falling onto my chair, Beethoven sonata through

the cloth webbing of our Philips radio. Solitude. Just like Saint Francis—
who I dressed as for an All Saints' Day school play, my tunic an old bed
sheet dyed brown, tied with white cord.

Brought up on pencil, I made the transition to pen, clunky
typewriter, portable Hermes, then a Macintosh Classic computer—
which I still use—a glorified typer that saves the donkey work of
whiteout, carbon paper, or re-typing an entire page for one lousy
correction. From my life as a kid right into shoe-scuffling "oldenhood,"
I've retained the idea my parents gave me: one goes out into the world
(alert, senses tuned), observes, feels, returns home, transforms mind-
body experience into words, illustrates what is written, makes book.
Implied was that one learned from the world, as well as about it, that
the journey reformed one's life as well as informed it.

Youngsters around me (never thought I'd be saying that) seem to
have grown up in cyber diapers. Electric fingers, digital eyeballs.
Pixelmania. If they notice me at all, they stare curiously—as if writing
were an act left over from a remote geologic age. Sometimes they tell
me, "Hope I'm still traveling when I'm your age." But often I hear a
hidden, "Gee, don't know if I want to be doing this when I'm his age."
Truth is, I haven't a clue to age. No mirrors in these cheap guest houses.
Anyhow, got better things to do than stare at my face on a wall. Sketch
a willow, sketch a gourd, spit on my writing brush and work it into a
point, run my jackknife over the curb and tweak the edge:

>sharpening pencils
>peeling mango, shaving whiskers
>with this little blade.

Traveling is a stay-young asana, hard-work routine. Opening the door to another continent is the same as going into my study. Don the editor's eyeshade. Press option caplock butterfly shift control. Return delete escape-button space bar. Hold the margins, flame the torch. Print look-alike laser last-draft first-try dogday rewind. Take pencil from ear, scribble universal seductive shapes of individuals within the inexhaustible mob. Stroll through modern women, balloon-headed profiteers, and deadbeats. Hawker over a pyramid of "Solar Toilet Paper." Cobbler under his "Scandal Maker" sign. Moralist and pickpocket sneaking off to count their change. Earth-grub farmyard types. Hip-swiveling prostitutes with removable eyelids. Transient infidel beauties chased by holy men strapped to beds of nails. Priest leaving the confessional with Lucifer's bags. Aunt Jemima talking it out with Dr. Hip. Chief Joseph briefing Malcolm X. Felix the Cat doing a little nasty with Minnie Mouse. Tathagata investigating third-eye Void. Prince of Lingering singing to William Blake under the jacaranda tree. All one world. Flags and Flatulence. Crap-shoot hipster and Avalokitesvara. Death penalty and Dalai Lama. Academics arguing the laws of existence. e.e. cummings dragging along his lowercase. Madman unbuttoning his fly. Beggar greasing his rollers. Trapeze lady walking civilization's flaming tightrope. Amputee measuring the progress of his missing limb. Jesus at it again with Mary Magdalene. Goofballs. Lovemilk. Ginko blossom. Waterbirds taking to the air after a passing Kawasaki.

Between the mob, give me ice peaks, desert hardpan, a zigzag trail over Zoji La, Siberian geysers, whirlpools in the Komodo Sea, a homesick ditch digger, the personal dignity of the farmer, Joan of Arc's sword, the soldier who refuses. Not the phony entrance exam, propped-up career path, requirements of the state, common sense of the nation—based on false evidence, vote tampering, nuclear proliferation, unilateral head shrinking, preemptive blowback. All beings the flawed mirror of the supreme being. No God but in things (made possible by the growing deficit of the credit machine):

> market lady bends
> to show me her ripest
> melons.

## 21 NOVEMBER: BANGKOK

### EMPTY PHENOMENA ROLLS ON
### DEPENDENT ON CONDITIONS ALL

Sign over a street vendor selling amulets, Mahathat Road. We stoop, inspect, sift through bronze, clay, wax, molded resin. I purchase a brass monk seated on a tortoise, Renée a clay Buddha dispelling fear—gifts for ones back home. Herb sellers and cure cranks line the sidewalk. Religious tapes and monks' umbrellas. Tallow, antimony, jasmine water, licorice, pine-flower pollen, a bottle of ball bearings, jar of rubbers. Grisly photos in one shop: this is how you'll look if you don't buy the right herbs. Patches of black fuzz erupting on necks and noses. Mustard-colored goiters bulging in ungodly places. Boulder-size testicles hanging like orioles' nests between legs. Jaws without teeth. Nipples larger than their breasts. Hair consuming a young girl's back. If your toes are too long, you can have them clipped off. If a mole's bothering you, there's a guy behind a portable curtain with a tray of Q-tips and battery acid.

An eerie old gentleman sits in front of one shop. He's smoking a cigar in an out-of-place European chair. Purple suit coat, sequined pants. Shriner's hat with floppy tassel. Medals hanging from lapels. Chevrons stitched to shoulders. Reminds me of life-like dummies of Maximón, the stogie-puffing healer-saint they splash with aguardiente in Guatemala. The man doesn't move, doesn't talk. He might be dead. Certainly he is not of this world. On either side of him are plastic parasols, ego-splitting sabers, key-chain goddesses, coin-operated whips, crystal bells, tin apsara wings, a bottle of blood, bundles of mint under a pair of false teeth, a fiddle without strings, long-necked spoons for turning babies in wombs, mechanical arm sockets, sponge-rubber falsies, packets of "Darkie Tooth Powder"—black men all in a row flashing white teeth under top hats.

mendicant's sign:
WORSHIPFUL MASTER
PLEASE DONATE

Few tourists here. No one caught in the rev of curiosity, nor giving themselves over to the in-and-out zoom lens that tongue-ties the brain. We amble with aimless vulnerability, subject to instant mind rearrangement, absorbing the weird surroundings. Like Alice through the keyhole, or Tom in the cave with a ball of string. No defense. Simply eager to be hit by what's in the ring. The road takes the top off my head, scuffs my already banged-up shoes. Every time I'm done with one of these ventures, I have to be rolled in medicinal leaves, left to steam, brought back to life by a deep-thrill back rub and a geography book to see where I've been. Get resettled, then take the knee-wracking descent into the journals, the back-breaking climb out, the mania to transcribe, put it in words, serve it hot to waiting guests. All 12 of them.

## 22 NOVEMBER: TO PRACHUAP KHIRI KHAN

Sunday morning taxi to Hualamphong Station. Sans the obstacle course of traffic, the city is pleasant. You can pick out details of architecture along streets normally lost in chaos. Tall green shutters, Naples yellow facades. Iron balconies erupting with flowers. A wooden building painted like a white envelope—the post office. Amber sun on white wicker chair. Beauty parlor with red eyelashes on baby-blue door. Lady rinsing aubergine, man rinsing motorbike. The taxi driver asks where we are from, how many hours by jet, and says it must be lonely to travel, lonely far from home. "But lonely make you want to find something live for. Lonely okay."

After numerous delays, waiting on the platform among arriving and departing trains, our train is finally ready. Conductor gives the okay, and we slowly roll down the line, south. Most tourists are headed to Surat Thani and the islands, but we'll deboard before that, in Prachuap Khiri Khan, a town visited mostly by Thais, noted for fresh, cheap seafood. It's on the gulf, facing some attractive karst islands. Good enough reasons to check it out.

daytime moon
everyone on the platform
watching the clock.

166

Before leaving Bangkok, I came upon Hugh Swift's *The Traveler: An American Odyssey in the Himalayas*. Hugh's photographs have always been dear to me; we've been to many of the same places, with the same eye. He was an odd-looking, poetic guy who repeatedly visited Asia, walked thousands of miles in India, Nepal, the Hindu Kush. Between travels, he met a strange and untimely death: he fainted on a sidewalk in California and never woke up.

Hugh pretty much traveled threadbare, taking to the loneliness of the road—camera and umbrella his only companions—in a kind of artistic and symbolic journey. He was willing to become vulnerable, let the act of travel shake his beliefs, rearrange his head and heart. The journey, in the tradition of those contradictory T'ang Dynasty "banished immortals," was an exercise in renunciation, an awakening to the joys of solitude, to others' lives, to another self. Inevitable bafflement, conflict, surprise, challenge—all part of it. Hugh had an inborn ability to take his time, to "get down" with complete strangers. Foot travel fine-tuned his senses, provided the materials of his art, a wealth of it to be found in ordinary life rather than in refined beauty. His approach to the road was that of a true minimalist: canvas knapsack, sturdy boots, compass, notebook, umbrella—no fancy fleece, running shoes, digital equipment, waterproof GPS.

Scanning *The Traveler*, I began to reflect on my own travels as a young man, largely fanned by the government trying to draft me out of the Peace Corps into the American War in Vietnam (Hugh was already there, teaching English as a conscientious objector). At home and abroad, young Americans were taking to extremes to protest the war and obligatory draft. A Peace Corps buddy stood in an Andean meadow and shot his trigger finger off. Another decided to grow sores and drink enough bad water to give him amoebic dysentery before being flown off—at taxpayer's expense—for his physical exam. One volunteer, tired of dealing with the military's constant pestering, gave up the fight to remain a peace worker, allowed himself to be drafted, and died in a war he never approved of:

> young warriors' blood
> dismissed on the news
> by men straightening their sleeves.

In my postal box, notice-to-report-for-induction orders arrived one after another. Peace Corps lawyers were helpless against Johnson's escalated war, and I was forced to succumb to the army's physical and written exams. Flown from Ecuador to the Canal Zone, I mocked the hearing test, was told to "Get out and move on!" by a cocky 20-year-old, then failed the written test, only to be approved for induction. How eager, how desperate they were!

Back in Ecuador, I asked if I could work in the Upper Amazon, where, within weeks, I received an auspicious invitation by a Shuar shaman (now largely replaced by trendy, quick-to-rise-to-the-occasion "healers") to participate in an ayahuaska ceremony. Naked, swimming a jungle stream after a night of vomiting out the Canal Zone, I decided to quit the Peace Corps and take to the road in a necessary, self-imposed exile. Hitching through Peru, Bolivia, and Chile (soon to be scourged and dismantled by the CIA-backed Pinochet coup), I looped back along the Andean spine, said adios to amigos in Ecuador, caught a ride with an anthropologist up through Central America and Mexico to Venice, California. Then Canada, then Alaska, to live. When the draft board caught up with me, it was back through 55-below Yukon, all the way to Mexico, to live. My father, a World War II vet, was amazingly supportive, even bought me a new set of tires. My mother was embarrassed and accused me of being "restless."

I never began my travels out of restlessness. Still don't. I crave my home, my nest, my woodpile, my garden—as much as I like to roam. In Burma, an astrologer once did my chart. I looked it over in the quietest refuge I could find in Rangoon: a bench in front of the monkey cage at the zoo. The configurations revealed a perfect balance between homemaker and wanderer, recluse and social being. Today, rattling along on this train to Prachuap Khiri Khan, clouds and fields out the window, I realize it's the same as it was then—I stay home because I love to dig the soil, hide in my studio, paint, write, peel shrimp, turn up the stereo, eat, drink, converse, make love, sit in silence. I travel largely for the same reason I sit in silence: to see what it brings up.

> along the tracks
> in a green field, a basket
> of white laundry.

The days are full of little pictures, enough so that imagination takes a back seat to reality. Curiosity and bewilderment are at the wheel, randomness and unpredictability in the driver's seat. Unless you stop wondering about it, open the door, and step into it, Southeast Asia remains predictably exotic, packaged by travel writers eager to entertain, tell dangerous tales, make it seem like they're the solitary adventurers bumping shoulders with strange people, braving countless dangers and annoyances to bring you the color and spice of "the orient."

Questions I'm asked about travel never seem to be: why do you travel, what do you do out there, who do you meet, what's your routine between waking and sleep? Rather, it's: how do you *do* it?—a question referring to financial means, often asked with as much envy as perplexity. The answers are deceptively simple. Don't have a job. Not in debt. Kids not depleting my meager income with college tuitions. No fear of unknown. Blessed with good health (no wood to knock on, so I'll knock on my head). No need for first-class airfare, Ex-Oficio clothing, five-star hotel, air-conditioned cocktails, private driver, etc.

Once, a friend mentioned to a mutually respected poet that I was off to the Himalayas. The reply: "Where does he get the money?" End of conversation. He was neither happy for me nor interested in why I'd chosen the destination. He probably wanted to be going to Nepal, too. But he was in line for a new teaching position, had social events to attend, and obligatory faculty meetings. I recall how he never liked trust-fund kids, welfare checks, or people who he assumed traveled for leisure or escape.

I've never been interested in defending my travels, but I sometimes wonder what I would have said to such a man. That I wasn't a trust fund hippy; never relied on grants (did garner a $10,000 NEA award one year) or the academy; always got by on a few bucks: cutting wood, selling a painting, giving a lecture, publishing an article, setting fenceposts, teaching as a poet in the schools; no big inheritance, but was blessed with a somewhat visionary, if not scrupulous, father who wished to die only after having left all his money to his three children while alive.

Dad—a bow of gratitude. Every few years toward the end of his life, he doled out modest increments of two to 5,000 dollars. He loved giving the money, watching what happened with it. And we loved receiving it. The first round I used for a down payment on a $54,000 house on the Rio Grande, near Albuquerque. Over the years, with lots of love and patience, I installed a new roof, floors, windows, native landscaping, and built an adobe studio. Never thought of real estate as investment—too busy patching things together to make ends meet. Still am.

One winter, a friend—trading-post operator, numerologist, math wizard, esoteric thinker, part-time realtor—printed out an amortization. Halfway through it, we tossed it into the fire, cracked a bottle of chianti, and laughed. Market value, yes; but what about practical and spiritual value? Richard asked: does the house allow you to make a living, do what you want in life? Of course! I nodded. Nestled in the cottonwoods, the house was a gift: a leafy, quiet retreat. Good walks, productive thinking. Before Albuquerque surrounded it, I knew every neighbor. People hadn't started selling off their chile fields; developers hadn't ravaged open space with tacky houses rented to newcomers who moved on when jobs gave out; Intel wasn't on the hill spewing toxins into the air, drying up the orchards, ruining people's health. I had ample space to write, paint, and prepare classes. The house, well lit and airy, allowed for maximum creativity. It was a place for my children to grow, and, when it came time to move to northern New Mexico, the house had, without me paying attention, appreciated. That's how it should be. Enough time between work to play. A little unexpected recompense for the sweat of each line, every stroke of the brush.

> through white haze
> nameless mountains
> washed with surf.

## 22 NOVEMBER: PRACHUAP KHIRI KHAN

Love in the afternoon. The big airy room rocks gently on its posts. Curious dragonflies bat against the screen. Voices filter up through banana leaves into silver sky. Oh trample on me! We laugh in damp sleep when fingers and flesh are through. Too hot for more phantom petting under the mosquito net. We become tender animals while shadows grow deep. A freighter somewhere off steers into the bay with a slovenly groan. Downstairs espresso machine fizzes triumphantly. Children bat plastic balls against the garden walls. Twenty to five.

Deboarding the train was a charge. We were the only ones to get off. In clear tropic sun, the quaint wood station met the eye like a child's toy, tilting this way and that. A Thai flag snapped and fluttered on its wooden pole; little concrete waiting benches curved up between evenly trimmed hedges; the station's yellow, shuttered windows were outlined in brown; a brass bell on the platform gave off heatwaves under moist puffs of sea cloud. A gate, arched with a sprawling pink bougainvillea, opened onto a shady street that curved downtown toward the sea. Ceremoniously, we ducked through and walked between two-story shophouses, weathered by wind and salt, a few freshly painted in incongruous pinks and greens. Women were taking down laundry from balconies over the shops below—pharmacy, hardware, software, newspaper stand, fishing tackle, optician, barber:

> any style hair cut
> for two dollars
> but I've got no hair.

Our hotel has every appearance of an old Chinese boarding house, one that might have catered to sailors, dockworkers, prostitutes. Now it serves, with astute cleanliness, the occasional farang or Thai businessman. If I spoke Thai I could learn the history of the place. As is, I must rely on guys like Kaka, not the fisherman with whom I'd love to hang out. There's a smattering of English spoken here, though, and the family is friendly and accommodating. To boot, there's fresh coffee in the morning. They grind the beans soon as they finish their 6 A.M. ritual offering of steamed rice to the barefoot monks who parade around town for alms.

## 23 NOVEMBER: PRACHUAP BAY

Crimson sky, aqua sea. Water birds circling two bobbing fishing boats at the pier, silhouetted in setting sun, slapping one another in rough waves. Sea gypsies unload their catch, speaking their own language, working with quick, easy rhythm. They wear loose, baggy-legged pants tied at the waists with sash-like extensions of cloth. Some wear rubber boots; others go barefoot, nimbly hopping nets and floats, boat to boat. Their powerful bodies ripple and shimmer with exquisite rhythm as they lift the catch from nets to trays to ice shoveler to the refrigerated trucks on the pier. Despite the heat, no one is sweating. Youth! I tire just watching their graceful swing of arms, the stretch of chests, backs, and abdominal muscles as they bring trays of crabs, squid, lobster, buckets of shellfish, and huge tuna over their heads. One muscular body to another, it all goes smoothly and silently amid the rocking boats, the creak and toss of wood, iron prongs, and pulleys. The light, the bodies, the composition, the physical beauty, the power—it's like a Géricault painting, or the photographs of Sabastião Salgado. After leaving the pier, we silently digest the exquisite imprint of the scene. We lament not having had our cameras. But, we saw and felt more without them.

A good sea breeze dries my sarong in 10 minutes. Someone's practicing Louie Armstrong beyond the breadfruit trees—"Dear Old South Land," ripe and bawdy through baby-blue shutters, mixed with a soundtrack of grackles, gulls, and popping motor scooters. I think of Cuba. Wavewash over Baracoa's shore front. That deep green sea. This one. Our kind of place.

The "Plern Smud" Restaurant, lapped by the bay, has us laughing at first, a good name for a post-modern Nadista grunge band. But it comes highly recommended so we take a seat and let the sea breeze soothe us as we sprinkle lime and chile over roasted cashews, order

Chang beer, two glasses, and a small bucket of ice. Thai style. Next comes a spicy tom yam kung soup, best we've had in Thailand. The cap mushrooms, lemongrass, coriander, and chile (three kinds) are absolutely fresh. There is something about eating sweet, succulent shrimp down south, sandwiched between two oceans (Gulf of Thailand and the Andaman Sea) that sharpens each sour, salty, hot flavor. Delectable citrus overtones, too. And that of cloves. Next, a round of "cuttlefish" (so says the menu)—squid marinated in fish sauce, bathed in roasted garlic and oil, lightly stir-fried, served with rice and sliced tomatoes. Another round of beer, and then: deep-fried prawn cakes, with thinly sliced cucumbers bathed in vinegar and fish sauce. Meanwhile, three other items on the menu catch our eye:

FRIED SPICY WITH FOREST PIGS
DANCING SHRIMP WITH SWAMP CABBAGE
GLASS NODDLE WITH PORK SINK

## 25 NOVEMBER: RANONG

West side of Thai peninsula. Tobacco-color sun filtering over Burma's tip. The country afar always more mysterious when seen from nearby. Downtown is narrow and crowded. Dark old places, Chinese script. Donuts bubbling in vats. Cybercafe named GODNET. Chess players outside lacquered temple. School kids upside down on monkey bars. Red-beard Muslims in white gowns vending cookware in rain-stained shops. HAPPY AFTERNOON, a market stall, serves strong Hokkein coffee filtered through a sock right into your cup. Tomorrow head south down Andaman coast toward Khao Lak, get a hut in the rainforest where we can stop for awhile, let thinking ebb into the sea, let where we've been wash in:

> asking directions
> three different ticket vendors
> three different answers.

## 27 NOVEMBER: ANDAMAN COAST

Smooth-bouldered coast dotted with islands and inlets, necks of jungle, riparian bird life along streams running their cold fingers into the warm sea. We'll bunk among lianas and tropical broadleaf trees, listen to the geckos, the chatter of kingfishers between the ocean's swell, the *twichk twichk twichk* of a songbird rapidly descending through the pines. Renée sees a flying squirrel, teases the crabs, sweeps the deck as she would at home. In the afternoon, a terrific storm crackles over the coast; rain wallops from steely thunderheads drawing furious moiré patterns over the metallic surf. We exit the water quickly, make for our hut, let the rain shower us off on the porch, yellow trumpet flowers breaking from vines, red hibiscus in a bowl between two glasses of tea. The sea, swollen by wind and rain, rolls and rolls, a blurry, liquid mystery—dream-like and frightening. Slowly, a distant spit recovers its clarity. Sun appears fuzzy gold behind a thick ladder of electricity bisecting the sky.

## 29 NOVEMBER: ANDAMAN COAST

The Germans on the beach today, what is it with these faces from so-called "civilized" countries? What makes them turn away when meeting another person? They seem to have forgotten something essential: how to smile. I suppose the Napoletano in me is over-sensitive to hard-drawn features that turn back into their weary pink shells at the sight of another human being. On the beach they want privacy. Into the night, they drink late. In the morning they offer no greeting, but start right in with their orders. We're only a couple of hours from Phuket, with direct flights to Europe; that might explain the scattered presence of these tourists who can't stop talking, smoking, viewing each other through camcorders, or rigidly holding to standards of how "their" Thais should serve them. As Rabindranath Tagore wrote: "Humility is when we come nearest to the great."

If that's so, most of us have a long ways to go. My journey suffers its biggest interruption when I fall on my face with judgment and expectation. The blather of tourists should be a signal not to react, but to remember the joys of solitude, the practice of silence. Bearing witness to arrogance should not give way to rant, but to the practice of kindness. That'd be the zen way: transform, transcend. Fan the ripple of goodness, watch it circle out into the world. Or, to lighten up a bit, Okakura Kakuzo:

> "Let us dream of evanescence
> and linger in the beautiful
> foolishness of things."

Too often I'm heartbroken, run ragged by the violent unpredictability of our human world: the hubris of blindly calculating leaders with big ideas that spawn big-death wars. Six billion people wrapped around the planet; everyone looks out from a different window. Traveling knocks the hard corners off one's usual perspective, takes the frame from the window, opens the glass to another's view. I'm not Buddhist, but the tiny, faceted lens I look through while in Thailand, is. The view begins in a dragonfly's eye, opens out to the rings of Saturn, the black holes of space, and returns into the deep well of the original self. The small self, no bigger or more important than anything else in the jeweled net of creation. Bashō was on the mark when he proclaimed: "The journey itself is one's home." The traveler discovers it quickly, going light, learning to listen, fine-tuning the pedestrian rhythm, experiencing luminous uplifts, dreary bogs, bits of exchange with commoners going about daily life. Playfulness, pathos. Insight, delight. Lost in dewy brambles, awakened from a nap by a passing cloud, seeing the moonrise in a ferry's wake, watching the temple abbot sweep around falling leaves, losing a favorite cap while experiencing mistaken satori on a speeding Yamaha. Gravity pulling stones from a mountain cairn. Rice fields soaking with reflections, stars where the feet should be. Curious, vulnerable, less certain, open to differences—that's to be at home in the journey.

> a slight breeze
> and the whole rice paddy
> shimmers with dew.

In America everything is big, except the computer chip. Big mugs, big cars, big schedules, big football games, big pills for big people, big flags over big malls, big talk from big sissies who run big business. Give me a twig fire. Cup of sake. Tea leaves unfurling in a clay pot. Narrow path through a parsley garden outside a willow shack. Chinese herb pills that slip easily down the throat. No smart bombs. No information bomb. No one going birth to death without chance revelation stirring the doldrums. I sometimes think America invented instant coffee, then sat down to avoid itself. Today, on a path to the beach:

> sunburst
> in grains of quartz
> from the sweeper's broom.

I'm not sure why things are bigger than they should be. Maybe when we got up off all fours our heads got fat. Poets are notorious for clawing the ranks, wanting bigger venues, bigger audiences, always working toward the top, when they should be growing greens at the bottom—where the richest soil is. Granted, a little recognition comes in handy; but a lot is bothersome. More recognition means you get a lot less work done. You're called out of your solitude for road tours, book signings, and publishing fairs where you're forced to ham it up, drink sour mash, do a little dance for the literary landlord. You might make it home with a little cash (enough to buy some extra shoelaces), a few stolen ashtrays (but who smokes?), a good-luck doorknob, a bunch of e-mail addresses of admirers who'll later hit you with the penultimate request (aptly summed up by Steve Sanfield):

179

"I've got eighteen inches
of unpublished poetry.
Want to have a look?"

Ah silence. Silenzio. Soledad. Sure, I want to talk late into the night—
with the right person (and she's right here beside me). Sure, I love to
keep quiet for days. Have time for poems, letters, snail trails, music, and
laughter. For clipping my toes, pulling wax from my ears, playing freeze
dance with the grandkids, mending the fence, fixing the space between
the rails. But the constant striving is to make light the load. Shred
information glut that makes mud of mind.

At home we rise early. On the Andaman Coast, even earlier. Watch
stars fade, sun light the bamboo. Listen to blue-tailed bee eaters, warblers,
whistling ducks. The lizard's throat goes *thump-thump-thump*. The waves
pound at disappearing shorelines. Wisps of lavender fog nestle in jade
coves. The snail gatherer's legs are white as the moon. In the evening,
we walk between clouds and rain, catch fireflies between the fingers,
grains of quartz and feldspar between the toes. Tide curls, the water
ebbs:

insects sing
from the arms of Kuan Yin
—*simplify, simplify.*

A friend, Bari Long, who went to Mongolia is doing just that. He
writes that he had a cabin built for $500. He stares across a lake to the

mountains of Siberia, blue sky, a horizon of green. He's translating bird calls in the brushwood, sorting out seeds, tracking furry creatures through the forests into Russia. He eats wind, bites icicles from the eaves to brew his tea. Looking down into the dust of humankind, he panfries New Year's donuts to chanting shamans, Indian ragas, Uzbek torch songs. He reads by candle, wonders about Tu Fu, repairs injured animals. But when he walks out into the doldrums of civilization, the stations are crowded, there are throngs of look-alikes. Rules, regulations, permission slips. All the roads have semaphores, every path is paved. Visiting China, he writes: "Dead rivers, cold windowless dorms, fog and pollution, the ever-present entry gate, another hundred yuan to become legal. The feeling of being restrained overshadows any joy of reaching a summit."

Face to face with crowds and conformity, days filled with bureaucracy, long waits for tickets and trains, he finally manages to arrive at a wild-animal breeding ground, "a place full of miserably kept pandas, golden monkeys, crested ibis, and moon bear. I could have cried a million times for them. Such fantastic animals in such poor cages while multi-million-dollar construction projects were everywhere underway."

Traveling deeper, he rises above coal smoke and human babble, spies the tracks of something small—a sable or marten disappearing into a snowdrift along the mossy steps of a mountain shrine. Suddenly elation, pleasure. A sense of contentment to mitigate the big, disappointing world. Further on, he asks the way from "the ghost of Han Shan, a hermit sage wearing topknot and robes." A feeling of transcendence overcomes him. He's broken through the chains, the gates, the corralling points where everyone's gathered, guided, rushed, heads turned toward the obligatory "sight," minds unable to remember what was seen. He's in the clouds, his boots are broken, his nose drips, his hands are red, and saliva runs from the corners of his mouth. But he's truly left the world for "one of those misty mountain, gnarled tree, temple, wandering monk landscape paintings, a pavilion with two arched bridges at the confluence of two rocky gorges—as in a dream."

> sleep in a farmhouse
> tonight, everything
> up to the wind.

Our friend dove deep, followed his truth, took a chance, made action of dream, let the compass needle spin off the dial. His words bring me to the idea of living a life of immediacy, spontaneity, the no-compromise inherent in the poem, the mad edge always present, a distant climb forever beckoning. Sweetness, voluptuousness. Secret rivers outside us, to match the ones within. Names that intelligence doesn't provide. Things worth knowing that can't be taught. After yesterday's storm, muddy water evaporates into clear mist. My mind isn't in my head, it's as large as the universe. I'll accept momentary enlightenment, but not in any larger-than-life, gilded temple. I need a ramshackle, driftwood palace:

> satori's right here
> caught in my chin stubble
> too close to see.

Renée and I walk the sand, picking up shells, stepping over dozens of tiny translucent crabs that dance to the water's edge, and retreat. Each of us is lost in thought, comfortably so, until we notice two sprouted coconuts slowly bobbing out to sea on the tide. Side by side, leaf flags fluttering, they wander playfully away, letting restless currents determine their course. The unbroken horizon of perfect blue—the vastness, the void—always causes us to ponder our beginnings (we each grew up by an ocean), our inescapable end. Neither of us likes to imagine life without the other, yet both of us know the inevitable: to meet is to begin to part. Whirlpools, undertow, switching currents—same moon above, no matter which way the wind pulls. What is important in this dream in between? The 18th-century Japanese poet Renseki brush-stroked this poem before he died:

> I cleansed the mirror
> of my heart, now it reflects
> the moon.

Our friend in Mongolia loves the practice of tracking wild creatures. I love stepping out of distractions/abstractions to track the immediate— the haiku practice. Quick-snippet, no-mind reality "takes" that refocus the eye on the everyday mystery of things: events charged with sudden significance sans meaning, metaphor, symbolism. From sun-warmed grass, rains vaporize. Through frangipani blossoms, a waft of pyre smoke. In the bed of a burnt-out army truck, a farmer begins his rice seedlings. Fed by the ancestor's graves, a gourd vine flowers in the breeze.

Between the haiku practice—little stepping-stones which inevitably bring me across unpredictable chaos into the solace of a quieter shore— I look for the longer, wordier missives where a correspondent bares his or her soul. What a rare and honorable act it is for someone to uncap a pen, place a thought, a woe, an ingot-hot revelation on paper; give significance to daily life; provide both a real and psychic portrait within the curve-ball journey we all fumble along on. Only a handful of true correspondents remain in my life, and they often approach the page as did Michelangelo his block of marble, bringing out hidden forms— joyous, poignant—from daily experience, letting the chisel slowly reveal some transient presence within the stone. It matters not the mood— cynical, exuberant, desperate, roaring in hellfire, juiced with new love— it's the on-fire intimacy, gut-grabbing doubt, deep-spiraling questions, exact details of things seen that provide a sanctuary where I can untie my boots, live for awhile, walk the labyrinth, take a plunge, bathe my brain, come up clean. And I wonder: why is it that letter writing didn't put on the gloves and have it out with e-mail? Why is the act of finding a nook to sit in when the light is just right, the idea of contemplation, the taking of pen in hand to create a ritual around thought all but disappeared?

> evening cool
> the sound of ink
> brushed across paper.

I take a seat to watch the sea. My chair isn't perfect, its shape a little raw. I like it that way. No sedentary upholstery to eat me up with overstuffed armrests. Heat and humidity, black clouds boiling upward, sea washing in and out with undertow of thought. Desire, regret, love, loss, all my errors, old failures, new ones—foaming, smashing around barnacled rocks. Red-nosed priests, playboy acolytes, pimpled concubines, arty profs. The pompousness of youth, the golden surfer, Mr. Hotrod with slicked-back hair, a party doll whose panties show when she twirls and jackknifes. Gorgeous fantasies, sewer-hole dares, peer-pressure high dives, late-nite scrapes, Looney Tune bomb drop. Pop-up fumbles, cool-whip sex bouts, psycho career path, awards cauldron boiling on the iron fire. Phew! Let the baggage fall to sea. Push aside soggy tea leaves at the cup's bottom, find the Goddess smiling all the time. Why write any of this down? I'll make a fist of flowers, give it to the sky. Find a place in the heart, live where warmongers can't. Make light of my poem, fly it into the froth. Drape a bathing suit on my skeleton, walk into the waves, see if I still float.

> between tangled grasses
> a wave-tossed stone
> polished clean.

## NOVEMBER FULL MOON: LOY KRATHONG

The ocean swells, rivers and streams run high. Tonight, under the fat moon, Thailand will celebrate the Festival of Lights. Loy Krathong honors the water spirits, marks the end of the northern monsoon, signals the start of the rice harvest. People flock to rivers and lakes to set to float (loy) candle lit banana-leaf boats (krathong) filled with flowers, incense, and coins. In Chang Mai paper lanterns decorate doorways.

Hot-air lanterns lift into the stars. In Mae Hong Son, lotus-shaped krathong attached to paper globes drift from a sacred hill. In Sukothai, terraces are decorated with flame; temples are lit with sound-and-light shows. All over the country there are parades, fireworks, beauty pageants, food feasts, and colorful booths with games for kids—toys, sweets, pens and scribble-pads for prizes.

Here, where the river courses a smooth bend from rainforest to sea, the locals set their delicate boats adrift into the confluence. We do it too, with instructions to "Make a wish and set your boat out. If the candle stays lit until it disappears, the wish will come true." It's a gala and solemn celebration, and we're glad to be part of it. The preparation of the leaf boats is quite time consuming; parading to the river and setting them afloat is brief. While making the krathong, one can meditate on the lotus flower (pure mind rising from muck), on the three incense sticks (insight, compassion, harmony), on Buddha's life, on the river goddess, Ganga. "Loy Krathong is when we apologize to the water for polluting her. We vow to keep ourselves clean, we send away the bad, we let new life enter the soul."

> slurping noodles
> hunkered close to the earth
> we dine with the sea.

# 1 DECEMBER: ANDAMAN COAST

Renée and I prepare to leave, thunderbolts flashing. We make love to the rocking surf, watch clouds turn peach in the madonna-blue sky, flares of raspberry deckling their edges. The sun lowers quickly, a disk of hammered bronze. On the water's edge, a string of fishing boats lights up to attract their prey. Rough sea today, kingfishers chattering nervously. Tonight we order sea bass in cashew sauce, Panaeng curry, rice, beers, pineapple-fritter dessert. The presence of water has been our medicine: sweet, salty, soft. On some days, the calm air so pleasant for walking would thicken with humidity. Parading thunderheads, steamy ropes of rain, furious bolts of electricity would send us hoofing for shelter. As the clouds moved off, we would let their aftermath of gentle, sifting moisture bathe us. The physical world gained a brief twilight dimension then: geckos called; swallows circled to feed; sea eagles hovered; an overpowering, metallic whine of insects erupted from the forest. Flycatchers were busy in the last light, and roosting waterbirds shook a prismed serenade of droplets from the trees.

In a week-old *Bangkok Post*, a quote from Mother Teresa: "We cannot do great things on this earth. We can only do small things with great love." I think of Bashō: "Journeying through the world, here, there, cultivating a small field." The last thing I paste into my journal is a pink bougainvillea petal on a square of gold foil, the kind a pilgrim pastes to a Buddha, a tree root, or to the smooth curve of a sacred stone. Renée joins me, smiling, after her morning walk. We stand hand in hand, face the sea, breathe in, breathe out. No more plans, not much to carry, we step across the stream, walk uphill to the thatch-covered bus stop, and wait for the Bangkok express:

>           yesterday's darkness,
>           today's full moon,
>           both over the horizon.

## POSTSCRIPT:

Thailand's Andaman coast was hard hit by the December 26, 2004 tsunami which originated 450 kilometers southwest, in Sumatra. One hundred sixty thousand people died in 11 Indian Ocean countries; five million were left homeless. Three months later, 50,000 were still at risk of disease or malnutrition. Thailand's dead reached 5,400; nearly 2,000 of them were visiting foreigners. The area described in these final pages was severely damaged, with many lives lost. The place where we spent our last days—on a bluff in the rainforest over an inlet—was mostly spared; there were no casualties. Devastation in surrounding villages was enormous.

Condoleezza Rice described the tsunami as "a wonderful opportunity" that "has paid great dividends for us." In Thailand a group called Thailand Tsunami Survivors said that for "businessmen-politicians, the tsunami was an answer to their prayers, since it wiped coasts clean of communities that previously stood in the way of their plans for resorts, hotels, casinos, and shrimp farms." The new form of colonialism is reconstruction. Find a bombed country (bomb one if there isn't any), or one devastated by natural disaster, grab hold of the situation, direct global relief funds to a privileged few, hand over "relief tasks" to foreign corporations. Bring in the World Bank, who instead of prioritizing emergency aid for fishing villages (more than 80 percent of the tsunami's victims), will push for the expansion of tourism, industrial fish farms, privatized airports, beach playgrounds, etc. Move the homeless people inland, into "temporary" prefab boxes—and leave them there. Rebuild, reshape the coast as it wasn't. Industrialize, privatize, corporatize.

*The Rise of Disaster Capitalism*, Naomi Klein's alarming report in the May edition of *The Nation*, is a wake-up call to what's behind the facade of White House "disaster relief," as well as its "post conflict" plans for more than two dozen countries which, as yet, are not in conflict. The machine's teeth are bared. Bechtel, Halliburton, the World Bank, the International Monetary Fund are just getting started. The blade is down, the scrapers screaming forward. Do we stand in front of them, or listen to the words of Lew Welch? "We remain alert so as to not get run down, but it turns out you only have to hop a few feet to one side and the whole huge machinery rolls by, not seeing you at all." Which is what those hermit monks of ancient China did. Which is why the people of Rio Arriba County, New Mexico, where I finish these notes, have left a painted portrait of Emiliano Zapata standing tall on a roadside billboard: TIERRA O MUERTE!

*John Brandi, on the road, 1966*

John Brandi has been faithful to the craft of poetry, painting,
journaling, and gardening for the majority of his life. A recipient of
numerous awards, including an NEA poetry fellowship, he is an
ardent traveler, with over 30 books published in the U.S.
and abroad. His paintings and collages have been
featured in one-person exhibits and
are in collections worldwide.

*Kali is one of the fiercer aspects of the great goddess*
*Devi, the most complex & powerful of the goddesses.*
*As Shiva's consort, she represents female energy. Her four arms*
*signify the four directions of space identified with the complete cycle*
*of time. While symbolizing the power of time, Kali is also beyond*
*time, beyond fear . . . her giving hand shows she is the giver of bliss.*
*Because she depicts a stage beyond all attachment, she appears*
*fearful to us. So, she has a dual aspect—both destroyer*
*of all that exists & the giver of eternal peace.*

THIS IMAGE IS FROM DRAWINGS BY WOMEN OF MITHILA, INDIA